THE
ARTISANAL
KITCHEN

HOLIDAY
COCKTAILS

ALSO IN THIS SERIES

The Artisanal Kitchen: Perfect Pasta

The Artisanal Kitchen: Perfect Pizza at Home

The Artisanal Kitchen: Vegetables the Italian Way

The Artisanal Kitchen: Holiday Cookies

The Artisanal Kitchen: Party Food

THE
ARTISANAL
KITCHEN

HOLIDAY
COCKTAILS

The BEST NOGS, PUNCHES,
SPARKLERS, *and* MIXED DRINKS
for EVERY FESTIVE OCCASION

NICK MAUTONE

ARTISAN | NEW YORK

CONTENTS

INTRODUCTION 7

-1-
HOME BAR BASICS
10

A FOCUS ON BALANCE 12
THE RIGHT TOOLS 13
THE RIGHT TECHNIQUES 17
THE RIGHT GLASSWARE 19
THE RIGHT BOOZE 24
OTHER INDISPENSABLE ITEMS 31
MEASUREMENTS AND CONVERSIONS 32

-2-
PUNCHES
34

AUTUMN PUNCH 36
POMEGRANATE PUNCH 39
WHISKEY AND GINGER PUNCH 40
BANANA RUM PUNCH 41

-3-
BUBBLIES
44

CHERRY SUGAR FIZZ 47
MAGNIFICENT MIMOSA 48
FRENCH 75 51
BLOOD ORANGE SPARKLER 52
KIR ROYALE 54
PARK AVENUE 55
THANKSGIVING SPARKLER 56
BRANDYWINE SOUR 59
PEAR, POIRE 61

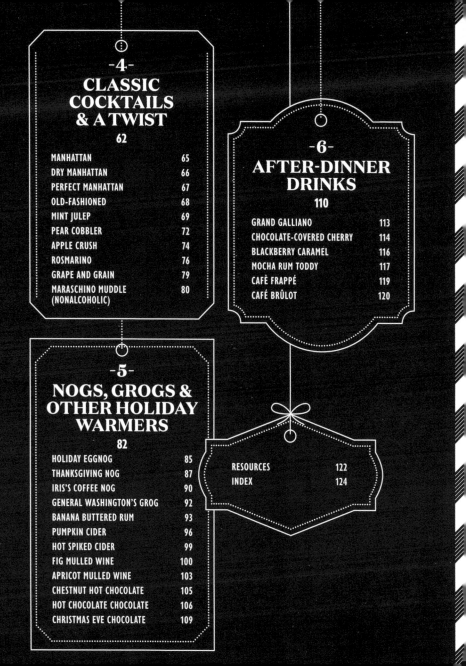

-4-
CLASSIC COCKTAILS & A TWIST
62

MANHATTAN	65
DRY MANHATTAN	66
PERFECT MANHATTAN	67
OLD-FASHIONED	68
MINT JULEP	69
PEAR COBBLER	72
APPLE CRUSH	74
ROSMARINO	76
GRAPE AND GRAIN	79
MARASCHINO MUDDLE (NONALCOHOLIC)	80

-6-
AFTER-DINNER DRINKS
110

GRAND GALLIANO	113
CHOCOLATE-COVERED CHERRY	114
BLACKBERRY CARAMEL	116
MOCHA RUM TODDY	117
CAFÈ FRAPPÉ	119
CAFÉ BRÛLOT	120

-5-
NOGS, GROGS & OTHER HOLIDAY WARMERS
82

HOLIDAY EGGNOG	85
THANKSGIVING NOG	87
IRIS'S COFFEE NOG	90
GENERAL WASHINGTON'S GROG	92
BANANA BUTTERED RUM	93
PUMPKIN CIDER	96
HOT SPIKED CIDER	99
FIG MULLED WINE	100
APRICOT MULLED WINE	103
CHESTNUT HOT CHOCOLATE	105
HOT CHOCOLATE CHOCOLATE	106
CHRISTMAS EVE CHOCOLATE	109

RESOURCES	122
INDEX	124

INTRODUCTION

My approach to cocktail making—a focus on balance of flavor and respect for the ingredients that make a drink—is as intense as that of any chef, from when the ingredients are purchased to the moment a cocktail is served to one of my guests. The result must meet the same exacting standards as any dish served in a great restaurant. Unfortunately, too many bars, restaurants, and even people who entertain at home don't feel that way. This is not to say that cocktails must be complicated or difficult to make to be delicious. On the contrary, sometimes the simplest drinks are the most elegant and tasty.

Nothing gives me more pleasure than sharing a meal, a drink, and great conversation with friends and family. My approach to entertaining is straightforward: I plan my meals and beverages somewhat thematically. I like to match the before-dinner drinks to the meal and the wine to be served with it. I try to surprise my guests with new and different drinks at unexpected times. I keep a well-stocked bar at home so I can usually accommodate my guests' imbibing pleasures. I prefer to plan out an occasion, including the drinks everyone will have, in advance. As my guests arrive, we share drinks perfectly matched to our evening. Then we move on to the meal, for which I will generally open a good bottle of wine during the first course. While cocktails are a passion, I adore wine with my meals and feel that this is a natural progression for a great dinner. At this point my guests will have finished their before-dinner drinks and had some food, so they can easily switch over to wine, which allows me to spend more time with them.

In order to accommodate all of your guests' particular preferences, you should always keep some basics on hand. For liquors, keep your favorite brands of vodka, gin, whiskey, rum, tequila, brandy, sweet and dry vermouth, and curaçao always at the ready. For extra ingredients, keep olives, seltzer, club soda, tonic water, bitters, superfine sugar, and kosher salt on hand. Of course, there are hundreds and hundreds of liquors, cordials, and brandies that you could stock, but these basics and extras make literally hundreds of different drinks to satisfy your guests' cravings.

The rules for pairing wine with food apply to cocktails as well: the cocktail should offer a counterpoint to the dominant characteristics of the food. For example, match rich, creamy foods with cocktails that have bountiful acidity and are full-flavored. The acid cuts through the fats and cleanses the palate. Salty foods demand contrasting elements such as sweetness to balance out the salt. Most cocktails are served before dinner because they are perfect palate openers. Some cocktails are great after dinner, when they act as a digestif or even as dessert. I generally do not serve cocktails with the meal because as good as cocktails are, their place is before or after the meal, rarely during it.

When introducing a wine to your meal after your cocktails, always remember that balance is the key. Great wines (no matter what the price) act as a condiment. If you have served strong cocktails before dinner, try to serve a light wine such as a crisp Alsatian or New York Riesling with your first course. If your cocktails were light and the meal permits, you could enjoy a richer chardonnay with the appetizer. Remember, the idea is not to get people drunk but to enhance their meal.

One universal rule for enjoying company is to prepare as much in advance as possible. For drinks that have both an alcohol and nonalcohol base, mix each component of the drink in a separate container, without any ice, well in advance and store them sealed in the refrigerator. When your guests arrive, you can then mix the two in the correct proportions without any fuss. Even easier are drinks that can be mixed in one container, such as Manhattans (see pages 65, 66, and 67). If you are having a group over, prepare a pitcherful of Manhattans for eight servings, or even more, and store it tightly sealed in the refrigerator, without ice, until ready to serve. When ready, you can stir or shake one or two servings at a time, allowing you to efficiently serve drinks to order.

Whenever I make a large batch of a drink that includes muddled ingredients, I muddle the ingredients with a mortar and pestle or in a large bowl with a wooden spoon and then divide the ingredients evenly among the glasses. I also freeze my fresh-squeezed juices. If I am having a group over on Saturday, I may squeeze all the juices on Wednesday and freeze them immediately. Allow the juice to thaw in the refrigerator overnight before using. The freezing does not negatively affect the juice, and you are still serving a freshly prepared product that will improve the flavor of your drinks.

I have organized the chapters in this book thematically. There is a section of punch recipes perfect for entertaining a large crowd, bubblies for festive occasions, good old classic cocktails with some unexpected variations, hot drinks for winter gatherings, and drinks to serve after dinner in lieu of coffee or dessert. If you are looking for a drink based on a specific liquor, such as vodka, simply consult the index, where you will find the recipes organized by base liquor.

I hope you enjoy this book and use it to share many great days and nights entertaining friends and family.

HOME BAR BASICS

UNDERSTANDING THE BASICS is the key to being successful in any endeavor. Perfecting basic techniques and using superior ingredients and the proper tools are fundamental to creating an extraordinary drink.

THIS CHAPTER FOCUSES first on what is perhaps the most important element of a great cocktail: balance. Without balance, a drink might be too sweet, too sour, or even just too big, but it is easy to avoid these excesses and get a grasp on how a properly balanced drink should taste. Next featured are a few basic tools and techniques that facilitate efficient and fun cocktail making. "The Right Glassware" (page 19) will help you identify which glass in your cupboard is best suited to the drinks being served. And finally, "The Right Booze" (page 24) is a straightforward guide to stocking your liquor cabinet with a few well-chosen basics.

CONSIDER THIS CHAPTER a brief but thorough course in great cocktail making. Taking a little time with these home bar basics before tackling the recipes that follow will enhance your experience and improve your results, for on these pages are the necessary building blocks to transform you into a master home bartender, and that's when the fun really begins!

A FOCUS ON BALANCE

The first rule of cocktail making is that balance is everything. In imbibing, balance might be viewed as the ratio of acid to sweetness to alcoholic strength. In the case of wine, those that are too low in acid taste "flabby," wines that are too high in alcohol taste "hot" or medicinal, and wines that are too high in sugar or too low in acid or alcohol taste cloying. These same principles hold true for cocktails.

Determining balance in your drinks will also help you understand the characteristics of liquors and mixers. For example, some bourbons are sweeter than others. If you use them in an old-fashioned, you may require less sugar. Other bourbons are higher in alcohol, and when using them, you may choose to add more water. Certain recipes in this book recommend a specific brand of liquor for the distinct sweetness, dryness, or extra kick it provides.

Personal preference also comes into play when making cocktails. I generally like my drinks on the sweeter side. When I am out, I take the time to inform the bartender what my preference is, and when at home, I make my drinks according to my tastes. If you are a newcomer to mixing your own cocktails, I suggest you make the recipes in this book as they are written. Once you have tasted the drink, you can determine if you prefer it sweeter, stronger, or lighter.

Also important is the size of the final drink. Remember that bigger is not necessarily better. In fact, many of the recipes in this book have lesser yields, for drinks that are often as small as 3 ounces. This allows you to sip a perfectly made, balanced cocktail ice cold. If it were any larger, the cocktail would become warm and insipid before the drinker could finish it. The more cocktails you prepare, the more comfortable you will become with determining your own specific sense of balance.

THE RIGHT TOOLS

You don't need much in the way of expensive equipment to mix great drinks. There are many good inexpensive starter kits on the market that contain shakers, strainers, jiggers, bar spoons, and a paring knife. Aside from the household basics—a bottle opener, can opener, and corkscrew—here are some other tools you will need.

SHAKERS

There are two types of cocktail shakers: the cobbler shaker and the Boston shaker. Either one works well, although each has particular features that make it useful. Specifically, the cobbler comes in varying sizes, from 8 to 16 to 24 ounces and even larger. These variations allow for different drink sizes and some flexibility when presenting and serving cocktails. For the shaking and stirring technique, see page 17.

To use a cobbler, fill the base shaker with ice and the cocktail ingredients. Place the top on with the cap in place. Shake well, remove the cap, and strain the drink into a glass.

The Boston shaker is the one most bartenders use. It is a little more versatile than the cobbler but slightly more difficult to use. The Boston is composed of two glass or metal tumblers. One tumbler holds roughly 26 to 30 ounces. The other tumbler generally holds 16 ounces. To use a Boston, fill the smaller tumbler with the cocktail ingredients and ice. Place the larger tumbler on top and gently but firmly give it a tap or two to seal the two tumblers together. Hold the bottom of the smaller tumbler in the palm of one hand while pressing the larger tumbler with the palm of the other and shake vigorously. Invert the shaker on a counter so that the larger half is on the bottom. Hold the seal between the two pieces with one hand; two fingers should be on the one end and two fingers on the other. Hold firmly and, with the heel of your other hand, tap the rim of the larger tumbler. This should break the seal. Remove the smaller tumbler carefully. Place a strainer over the top of the larger tumbler and pour.

STRAINERS

The Hawthorn strainer and the julep strainer each serves its own purpose, and both are necessary if using a Boston shaker set. The Hawthorn strainer has a metal coil on its underside, and the julep strainer is solid metal with holes throughout. The Hawthorn is used for shaken drinks and works with the larger tumbler, and the julep strainer is used for stirred drinks and is used with the smaller tumbler.

JIGGERS

Jiggers are basically tiny measuring cups. The most common jiggers have a long handle with two cups of different sizes that measure 2 ounces or less, but my favorite jigger is a small, shot glass–size measuring cup with measurements ranging from ¼ to 1 ounce and their equivalencies in teaspoons, tablespoons, and milliliters all etched on its side.

COCKTAIL SPOONS

Cocktail spoons are used to stir a drink in a pitcher or shaker. The same rules apply to stirring as to shaking: stir until the outside of the shaker is frosted and beaded with sweat, ten to fifteen seconds.

NUTMEG GRATER

This tool is indispensable for garnishing drinks such as hot toddies or punches such as Whiskey and Ginger Punch (page 40) with freshly grated nutmeg.

KNIVES

For cocktail making, you will need a paring knife for cutting your lemons, limes, and oranges and a chef's knife for cutting large fruit such as pineapples.

CHANNEL KNIVES AND ZESTERS

A channel knife has a rounded or rectangular metal head with a small curved blade and a hole on either the side or the top. This is used for producing long citrus-peel swirls. A zester has a steel edge with five tiny cutting holes. When pulled across the surface of an orange, lemon, or lime, it creates strips of peel.

MUDDLERS

Bar muddlers are used for mashing fruit, sometimes with sugar, to extract juice. They are also used for bruising soft fruit, such as cherries, and herbs, such as mint. The best muddlers are made of soft, unvarnished wood and are generally 6 inches long with a flat end on one side.

JUICERS AND REAMERS

I strongly recommend purchasing a citrus juicer. Make sure to get a model that is large enough to handle grapefruit as well as lemons and limes. In addition, always keep a wooden citrus reamer on hand. It is great if you have to juice just a few lemons or limes.

COCKTAIL PITCHERS

Tall, elongated, and somewhat narrow, cocktail pitchers range in size from 1 to 2 quarts. Standard cocktail pitchers also come with a long glass stirrer. Gallon-size glass pitchers and several plastic pitchers with tight-fitting lids are also good to have on hand.

THE RIGHT TECHNIQUES

There are very few strict rules for mixing drinks, and with just a bit of practice you can easily master them all.

SHAKING AND STIRRING

When shaking your drinks, follow this simple but important rule: shake vigorously until the outside of the shaker is frosted and beaded with sweat. The shaker should be so cold that it is almost painful to hold. This will generally take ten to fifteen seconds. Most important, maintain a consistent and constant rhythm while shaking to ensure that the drink is mixed effectively.

As for shaking versus stirring, it is my opinion that drinks that are all or mostly liquor, such as a martini, should be stirred; drinks that contain juice, egg, or other heavy ingredients should be shaken. The simple reason for this is texture: in cocktails that are primarily or all liquor, stirring produces a more delicate texture; for juice-based or weightier drinks, shaking emulsifies the cocktail, ensuring a smooth, even texture.

For very weighty drinks or those based on fruit purees, a technique called rolling is the best method for mixing and can be done only in a Boston shaker. Rolling consists of pouring a drink back and forth between the two tumblers. This thoroughly combines heavy juices with other ingredients without producing a foamy texture that is unpleasant in these types of drinks.

MUDDLING

To muddle, place the fruit, herbs, sugar, or other ingredients to be muddled in the bottom of a large glass or shaker. Using the flat end of the muddler, firmly press and twist the tool, crushing and breaking down the fruit or herb to release as much juice and essential oil as possible. If bruising an herb, do not press quite as hard; you don't want to pulverize it.

RIMMING

Rimming a glass with sugar, salt, or spices ensures that every sip of the cocktail is a multilayered experience.

The key to proper rimming is to keep the granules on the *outside* of the glass. Too many granules on the inside of the rim mean that each time the drinker tips his glass, the garnish falls into the cocktail, eventually throwing off the balance of flavors in the whole drink. The *correct* method is to pour the sugar or salt onto a small plate, rub the juicy side of a wedge of lemon, lime, or other citrus fruit on the *outer* edge of the rim—not along the inside—and holding the glass at an angle, roll the outer edge of the rim in the salt or sugar until it is fully coated.

FLOATING

Floating is a technique that has both aesthetic and practical benefits. Brightly colored syrups, cordials, or cream may be floated on a cocktail, giving an attractive layered look to the drink and dividing the drink into two distinct levels in the drinker's mouth. To float one liquid on top of the other, place the bowl of a spoon upside down over the cocktail and pour the cream or syrup slowly over it, allowing the liquid to gently spread over the top of the drink.

THE RIGHT GLASSWARE

Feel free to improvise when it comes to glassware. While there is a glass for every type of cocktail and each one is designed to enhance a specific drink, it is just not practical to own them all. For example, an old-fashioned glass can easily double for a whiskey-tasting glass. The most important rule in glassware isn't about the glasses at all. It is about what you serve *in* the glass—a high-quality, freshly made, well-balanced beverage.

The illustrations on these pages highlight twenty different vessels for preparing and serving wine, cocktails, and straight spirits. While you do not need all of these, you should keep the following basics on hand: old-fashioned glasses, highball glasses, martini glasses, all-purpose wineglasses, champagne glasses, beer glasses, and perhaps dessert wine or port glasses.

1

OLD-FASHIONED *or* **ROCKS GLASSES**

These can range from 8 to 12 ounces and are used for spirits served over ice, or "on the rocks." Generally they are short and round or, in some cases, rounded squares.

2

HIGHBALL GLASSES

Tall and round, these are used for drinks containing soda as well as liquor. Most highballs hold 10 to 16 ounces of liquid. Collins glasses are even taller and narrower and are often frosted.

3

COCKTAIL *or* MARTINI GLASSES

These are used for cocktails served "up," or without ice. Holding the glass by its long stem prevents the heat of your hand from warming the drink. Cocktail glasses can be as small as 3 ounces and as large as 10 ounces.

4

ALL-PURPOSE WINEGLASSES

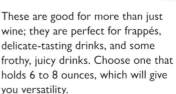

These are good for more than just wine; they are perfect for frappés, delicate-tasting drinks, and some frothy, juicy drinks. Choose one that holds 6 to 8 ounces, which will give you versatility.

5

CHAMPAGNE GLASSES

Though these come in a variety of styles and sizes (such as coupes, pictured on page 50), I prefer a champagne flute that is shaped like an elongated wineglass. This versatile style is great for serving sparkling wine as well as cocktails made with it. Choose a champagne glass that, like the all-purpose wineglass, holds 6 to 8 ounces to accommodate either sparkling wine or a cocktail.

6

BEER GLASSES

These can be as varied as wineglasses. The two shown here are a beer mug and a pilsner glass. A tall, heavy-bottomed beer mug is the most practical choice. Choose one that holds at least 12 ounces, the average size for a bottle of beer, and not more than 16 ounces, which gives you room for a big head on your beer or for ice if you are using the glass for another type of drink. A pilsner glass's footed bottom and elegant stemmed shape are perfectly suited to lighter, crisper beers, as well as for serving effervescent cocktails.

7

DESSERT WINE GLASSES or PORT GLASSES

Used for sweeter after-dinner wines and cordials, these glasses, which resemble a small wineglass, are also great for whiskey sours and other elegant frothy drinks served "up."

8

WHISKEY-TASTING GLASSES

These are specialty items used to serve whiskeys neat or straight and unchilled. In some respects, they act like a brandy snifter (see page 22). The bulbous bottom aerates the whiskey and allows the volatile vapors to dissipate.

9

BORDEAUX or CABERNET GLASSES

These are used for full-bodied and tannic red wines, such as Cabernet Sauvignon, the most common grape variety in Bordeaux. The rounded bottom and elongated top and shoulders allow the wine to aerate and "soften." This means that the harsh tannins and acids dissipate while the fruit and softer tannins remain.

10

BURGUNDY or PINOT NOIR GLASSES

Lighter, softer red wines need to develop their aromas, which dissipate too quickly. Therefore, these glasses are very wide at the bottom, then turn inward at the edge to trap and heighten the aroma of the wine, allowing the perfume of the lighter grapes to stay in the glass and not aerate too quickly.

11

MONTRACHET GLASSES

Full-flavored and full-bodied white wines such as Montrachet, Chablis, and California chardonnay benefit from the wide, open shape of these glasses, which allows air to enter and soften the acidity while enhancing the fruit.

12

AROMATIC WHITE WINE GLASSES

These are used for slightly sweet or fruit-forward wines such as Riesling that do not need to aerate. These smaller glasses keep the focus on the freshness of the wine, and the outward angling of the edge lets the wine hit the tongue in just the right spot for our taste buds to sense sweetness.

13

BRANDY SNIFTERS

These specialized glasses enhance the flavor and aroma of fine Cognacs, Armagnacs, and brandies. The wide, bulbous bottom allows a great deal of air to hit the brandy, softening the harsh alcoholic vapors and enhancing the caramel notes in the brandy.

14

SHERRY COPITAS

Very similar to port glasses but slightly taller and narrower, these glasses enhance the delicate aromas of sherries, allowing their complex scents and flavors to gently scoot up the glass.

15

GRAPPA *or*
EAU-DE-VIE GLASSES

These enhance the pronounced and assertive flavors of grappa with their tall, narrow shape. The glasses are generally small in volume, typically around 3 ounces. This glass also makes a very acceptable cordial glass.

16

**IRISH COFFEE
MUGS**

These are perfect for all manner of coffee drinks, nogs, grogs, and other hot beverages.

17

**HURRICANE
GLASSES**

These are shaped like hurricane lamps, typically hold around 15 ounces, and are ideal for tropical drinks.

18

TALL COOLER *or*
ICED-TEA GLASSES

These hold 16 to 20 ounces. They are wonderful for tall frothy and fizzy drinks.

19

PUNCH BOWL
and **PUNCH CUPS**

Punch bowls and larger vessels holding a gallon or more allow for a large volume of punch for serving.

20

**LARGE
PITCHER**

Large pitchers are the best vessel in which to one-batch drinks for parties.

THE RIGHT BOOZE

When stocking your bar, start with the basic spirits: vodka, gin, whiskey, rum, tequila, brandy, sweet and dry vermouth, and curaçao. From these you can make literally hundreds of great cocktails.

Do not use price as your only guide in choosing liquor for your home bar. Price alone does not ensure quality. Tasting as many brands of liquor as possible is the best way to decide what you like. Within each category of liquor there are many different styles. Scotch, for example, can be either blended or single malt, and its flavor can range from smooth to smoky to salty. Moreover, within these styles the level of alcohol can vary. Bourbon is a great example of this: it comes in 86-proof versions as well as in 101-proof versions. (Proof is the measure of alcohol in liquor, and the number is always double the percentage of alcohol. In other words, if a liquor is 80 proof, it is 40 percent alcohol.) Both are great, but they appeal to different people for different reasons.

VODKA

Vodka is a rectified spirit (distilled three times) produced from grain or potatoes. Ninety percent of the vodka produced is grain based. Occasionally, and mainly in Europe, rice or molasses is used. Though colorless and odorless, vodka has a subtle taste. I find that potato-based vodkas, such as Luksusowa from Poland, have very distinctive flavors. Some vodkas are distinguished by their texture, which ranges from oily to watery.

GIN

Gin is a distillate of cereal grains, especially corn and barley, although wheat and rye are also used. It is distilled three times (rectified), and during the distillation process, aromatic herbs and spices called botanicals are infused into the base neutral spirit. All gin includes juniper, and most gins contain six to ten different botanicals (like coriander, angelica, orange peel, cardamom, etc.).

The two most prominent styles of gin are Dutch and London dry. Dutch gin is 70 to 80 proof (35 percent to 40 percent alcohol) and is made from rye, corn, and barley and distilled in pot stills and aged in oak casks. This gin is excellent on its own or as a mixer. London dry gin is higher in alcohol than Dutch gin. The botanicals are added during the distillation process when the base spirit is actually in a vapor form before recondensing. This is a perfect martini gin or great as a mixer.

WHISKEY

Whiskey comprises a large, diverse family of spirits. Whiskeys are defined by several factors, including their three basic ingredients: grain, yeast, and water. Within these three ingredients are many variations that create a diverse array of end products. The type of yeast or base grain (corn, barley, rye, or wheat) and the water source have a dramatic effect on taste.

IRISH WHISKEY is based on malted barley and sometimes rye. Malting is a process by which the grains are allowed to partially germinate, thereby converting the natural starches to sugar, which in turn changes to alcohol. The malted grains are dried in a kiln before mashing and fermenting. The whiskey then undergoes its three-part distillation. After distillation, it is aged in casks until the desired house style is achieved.

SCOTCH goes through the very same process, with one exception: the malted grain is dried over peat fires, which give scotch its signature smoky profile. Scotch is often aged in old bourbon or sherry casks, and in some cases certain distilleries use both. These used barrels impart much subtler flavor than new, unused casks. Irish whiskey tends to be a bit mellower and sweeter than scotch, which has more bite and that smoky note.

BOURBON, which derives its name from Kentucky's Bourbon County, is made primarily from corn—up to 80 percent of the mash is corn, with the balance rye or wheat. The mash in any one bourbon is either of two types: sweet mash, a fresh mashed grain to which yeast is added to kick off the fermentation, or sour mash, which uses the residual mash from the prior fermentation to kick off the next batch. After fermentation, the base is distilled three times and allowed to age in new charred oak barrels. The charring of the barrels gives bourbon its smoky-sweet nose, and their being new adds to the pronounced sweet and sometimes vanilla notes in the resulting whiskey. Tennessee whiskey is similar in every way to bourbon except one: it undergoes filtration through charcoal before being aged in the charred oak barrels. This filtration process takes at least ten days.

RYE WHISKEY is made with a minimum of 51 percent rye by law. It is similar to bourbon but has a more pronounced savory, spicy note.

RUM

RUM is made from molasses, sugarcane juice, or cane syrup. There are three basic kinds of rum: light-bodied, medium-bodied, and heavy-bodied. Light-bodied rum, also called white or silver, is aged for up to one year in casks and is filtered before bottling, which makes the rum fairly neutral. Medium-bodied rum, often called gold or amber, is aged in wood longer than light rum and often has added caramel for even color. This rum is richer and smoother than light rum. Heavy-bodied rum has two distinctly different subcategories: blended rums and well-aged sipping rums. Blended rums are dark and heavily colored and have a distinct weight in the mouth. The well-aged sipping rums are kept in casks much longer than all other rums and take on a brandylike flavor; they can be sipped on their own or mixed in drinks. Rum is produced all over the Caribbean and West Indies, with each island producing its own distinctive rums. Have some fun and treat yourself to an island comparison.

TEQUILA

Tequila, an interesting, delicious spirit, is made from the heart, or *piña*, of the blue agave cactus. Mexican law very strictly regulates the different categories of tequila, the main two of which are mixto and 100 percent agave. Mixto, as it sounds, is a mix: 51 percent agave mash and up to 49 percent other sugars, such as cane or beet; 100 percent agave is distilled solely from the blue agave plant. Within both mixto and 100 percent agave, there are four main subcategories: *blanco, joven abocado, reposado*, and *anejo*. *Blanco*, white, silver, and *plata* all mean the same thing: tequila that is aged fewer than sixty days in wood. *Joven abocado* is also known as gold tequila. The color comes from other flavoring and coloring agents. *Reposado* means "rested" in Spanish. These tequilas must age at least sixty days in wood, and many are aged at least a year; they can also have flavoring and coloring agents. *Anejo* means "aged," and by law it must spend at least a year in wood, though most actually spend a longer time. One hundred percent agave *anejo* is my favorite tequila. It has pronounced complex and earth notes, and while it has a bite, the extra aging in wood mellows the sharp or bitter tones.

BRANDY

Brandy is a broad term, encompassing a large family of spirits that includes many different and distinctive types. It is basically the fermented and distilled juice of grapes, apples, pears, plums, peaches, or almost any other fruit grown. More often than not, when we say *brandy*, we are referring to grape brandy, as that is the most prominent of all brandies. Any other type will be referred to by its fruit, such as apricot brandy, or by its stylistic name, such as calvados, which is apple brandy from Normandy, France. All brandies can be used in cocktail making, and you will see a variety of grape, apple, and other fruit brandies called for throughout this book.

Grape brandies are produced in many countries and in many styles, with the largest producers being France and Spain. Grape brandy starts out as wine, which is distilled and then aged in oak. It is blended, adjusted with water to the correct alcoholic strength, and often enhanced with caramel or other agents to produce a consistent house style.

In France there are two main types of aged grape brandies: Cognac and Armagnac. The differences are actually quite pronounced.

COGNAC, based on a wine made from the ugni blanc grape, is distilled twice in pot stills and then aged in new white oak casks from the Limousin and Tronçais forests in France. It is aged and blended in a slow process that marries small proportions of older stocks with younger stocks to produce a consistent house style.

ARMAGNAC starts as a blended wine made mostly from the ugni blanc grape along with a variety of other grapes local to southwestern France, where the brandy is produced. It is distilled in a continuous still and is aged in black oak casks from the Monlezun forest.

SPANISH BRANDY is often a better value than other brandies on the market—half the cost of an equivalent bottle of V.S.O.P. Cognac. The quality is generally high and the flavor quite unique. Spanish brandies are made in the solera system, a complex method that is used to produce all the wonderful brandies and sherries from Spain. New brandy is placed in barrels in the front of a row or on top of a stack. Each year, small amounts of older brandy are added to the new, and sometimes some of the newer brandy is added to the barrels of older brandy.

CALVADOS is apple brandy from the Normandy region of France. Fermented apple cider is double distilled, then aged in wooden casks. It must spend at least one year in cask, and the average for good calvados is ten to fifteen years. Many are aged as long as thirty, forty, or fifty years. In the United States, we have a great apple brandy called applejack.

VERMOUTH

Vermouth is a fortified and aromatized wine. The name comes from the German word *Wermut*, which means "wormwood," a plant that has a narcotic effect and was used in the early blends of many beverages—in general it is no longer used. Vermouth is made by infusing a base wine with roots, herbs, flowers, and even bark along with brandy and unfermented grape juice for sweetener. The mixture is then pasteurized, cold stabilized to remove impurities, filtered, and bottled. There are many different styles of aromatized wines and vermouths. Some are great for mixing, such as the basic sweet and dry vermouths. Others, such as Lillet or Dubonnet, Punt e Mes, and Carpano Antica, can also be served chilled on their own as an aperitif.

CURAÇAO

Curaçao comes in several different guises, and in any form, it is indispensable to the home bar. Orange curaçao is a cordial made from the bitter oranges of the Caribbean island Curaçao. It was originally produced in France and is now made all over the world. Cointreau, a French liqueur, is widely considered the best curaçao on the market. Triple sec, mentioned throughout this book, is a type of curaçao. For the most part, curaçao is used as a sweetener and flavoring agent for cocktails; it is almost never drunk neat.

OTHER INDISPENSABLE ITEMS

BITTERS

One hundred years ago a cocktail would not have been a cocktail without the addition of bitters, an infusion of alcohol, herbs, spices, fruits, and roots. Bitters were, and are, indispensable to great cocktail making. Apothecaries throughout the country used to make their own bitters, and all claimed theirs to be "the tonic to cure what ails you." Bitters can be categorized into four general types: aromatic, citrus, fruit, and herbed. Angostura and Peychaud's (both aromatic bitters) and citrus bitters are the most popular. The three are quite different and not necessarily interchangeable. All are great balancers in a cocktail.

ANGOSTURA BITTERS are the most widely used bitters among the three. They are also the darkest and most strongly flavored. The flavor of Angostura bitters is strong and herbaceous, with great acidity, just a hint of sweetness, and, of course, an appealing bitterness.

PEYCHAUD'S BITTERS have a distinctive cherrylike flavor and go particularly well with rum and sweeter cocktails for balance. They are of medium weight and color, compared to Angostura bitters.

CITRUS BITTERS' light color and sublime flavor are unique and complement the other categories of bitters. Given the diverse flavor profile and base ingredients, citrus bitters are subtle and alluring, enhancing many unique and vibrant cocktails.

MEASUREMENTS
AND CONVERSIONS

Most recipes in this book measure liquids in ounces, which is common practice when mixing drinks. Use the chart opposite to find the equivalent for measurements; they are rounded off for ease of use.

A NOTE ABOUT IMPERIAL MEASUREMENTS
If converting the measurements called for in this book to imperial, or British, measurements, note the following:

1 U.S. cup = 8 ounces
1 imperial cup = 10 ounces
1 U.S. pint = 16 ounces
1 imperial pint = 20 ounces
2 U.S. tablespoons = 3 imperial tablespoons

Adjust the measurements called for in this book downward accordingly when preparing these recipes using implements based on the imperial system.

LIQUID
(VOLUME)

AMERICAN	IMPERIAL	METRIC
⅛ tsp (1 dash)		
¼ tsp		1.25 ml
½ tsp		2.5 ml
1 tsp		5 ml
½ Tbs (1½ tsp)	¼ fl oz	7.5 ml
1 Tbs (3 tsp)	½ fl oz	15 ml
1½ Tbs (4½ tsp)	¾ fl oz	
2 Tbs (⅛ cup)	1 fl oz	30 ml
3 Tbs	1½ fl oz	45 ml
3½ Tbs	1¾ fl oz	
¼ cup (4 Tbs)	2 fl oz	60 ml
⅓ cup (5 Tbs)	2½ fl oz	75 ml
⅜ cup (6 Tbs)	3 fl oz	90 ml
½ cup (8 Tbs)	4 fl oz	125 ml
¾ cup (12 Tbs)	6 fl oz	175 ml
1 cup (16 Tbs)	8 fl oz	250 ml
1½ cups	12 fl oz	350 ml
1 pint (2 cups)	16 fl oz	500 ml
3 cups	24 fl oz	750 ml
1 quart (4 cups)	32 fl oz	1 liter
1 gallon (4 quarts)	128 fl oz	4 liters

SOLID
(WEIGHT)

US/UK	METRIC
½ oz	15 g
1 oz	30 g
2 oz	55 g
3 oz	85 g
4 oz	110 g
5 oz	140 g
6 oz	170 g
7 oz	200 g
8 oz	225 g
9 oz	250 g
10 oz	280 g
11 oz	310 g
12 oz	340 g
13 oz	370 g
14 oz	400 g
15 oz	425 g
1 lb	455 g

CHAPTER
-2-

PUNCHES

PUNCHES ARE AN EXCELLENT WAY to entertain large numbers of guests. Often colorful centerpieces at a party, punches make any occasion more festive, and the fact that they simplify your entertaining is purely a bonus. Almost anything can be converted to a punch—within reason, that is. A large bowl of a strongly alcoholic mixture may well kill the party before it begins. But certainly feel free to experiment. All you have to do is mix a spirit or sparkling wine with juice in a large bowl and you have a punch. Just remember that the ingredients should compose a mix that works well with both your meal and your tastes. When making these recipes or creating your own, avoid the urge to make them stronger by adding more liquor—punches, like any cocktail, should be balanced. The sweetness of most punches sometimes masks the alcohol, making it seem, by taste anyway, as if they contain less alcohol than they actually do. While the term "packs a punch" might seem as though it fits in this chapter, punches should above all be refreshing, with a good kick but not over the top.

AUTUMN PUNCH

MAKES TWELVE 7½-OUNCE SERVINGS

This cocktail is rich and weighty enough to stand up to a range of foods while still being effervescent and refreshing. It calls for Pedro Ximénez sherry, which is one of the world's greatest dessert wines. Thick, black, syrupy, and absolutely delicious, this sherry can be found at well-stocked wine shops. Look for Pedro Ximénez sherry made by Alvear or Lustau.

FOR THE CANDIED GRAPEFRUIT PEEL

2 GRAPEFRUITS

24 OUNCES WATER

2 CUPS SUGAR

2 WHOLE STAR ANISE (OPTIONAL)

FOR THE PUNCH

TWO 750-MILLILITER BOTTLES SPARKLING WINE, CHILLED

8 OUNCES PEDRO XIMÉNEZ SHERRY, OR MORE TO TASTE, CHILLED

12 WHOLE STAR ANISE, FOR GARNISH (OPTIONAL)

GLASSWARE

PUNCH BOWL
(SEE PAGE 23)
and
CHAMPAGNE GLASSES
(SEE PAGE 20)

PLANNING AHEAD
The candied chilled grapefruit peel must be blanched three times, simmered for about 3 hours, and chilled for at least 30 minutes. The candied peel can be stored with its syrup in an airtight container for up to 2 weeks in the refrigerator. Chill the sparkling wine and sherry for at least 30 minutes before finishing the punch.

To prepare the candied grapefruit peel, juice the grapefruits and set the juice aside in the refrigerator. Pull or cut away the fruit from the peel, taking care to keep the pieces of peel as big as possible and retaining the white pith.

Discard the fruit or save for another use.

Bring a pot of water to a boil and fill a large bowl with ice water. Blanch the peel in the boiling water for 30 seconds, then shock it in the cold water. Repeat two times, using fresh boiling water and ice water each time to remove any bitterness.

Meanwhile, place the 24 ounces water, the sugar, and 2 star anise, if using, in a medium-large nonreactive saucepan and stir to moisten the sugar. Bring to a gentle boil over medium-high heat. Reduce the heat and simmer until the sugar is completely dissolved and the syrup is slightly thickened, 3 to 5 minutes. Add the blanched rinds to the syrup and simmer over low heat for about 3 hours, until the syrup and rind are both a dark caramel pink color and the rinds are easily pierced with a knife and have a sweet-tart flavor.

Let the syrup and grapefruit rinds cool at room temperature, and then chill thoroughly before proceeding.

To prepare the punch, remove the candied peel from the syrup and cut it into long, thin strips. Set aside 2 to 3 dozen strips. Transfer the remaining peel and 8 ounces of the syrup to the punch bowl. Pour in the sparkling wine, reserved grapefruit juice, and sherry and stir gently until mixed. Taste and add more sherry if you prefer it sweeter.

To serve, place several of the reserved grapefruit strips in the bottom of each champagne glass and ladle the punch over them. Place a star anise on top, if desired.

TRICK OF THE TRADE
Instead of candying the grapefruit peel yourself, make the syrup as above, replacing 8 ounces of the water with 8 ounces grapefruit juice. Add 1 or 2 pounds of store-bought candied grapefruit to the syrup and simmer on low until the grapefruit is warmed through and softened, 5 to 10 minutes.

POMEGRANATE PUNCH

This is a great winter punch to serve when blood oranges are in season. The bright colors and complementary tanginess of pomegranates and blood oranges make them an ideal combination. Full-flavored yet light in body and texture, this punch is not overly filling and is thus a very refreshing aperitif to a rich winter meal.

1 LARGE POMEGRANATE

32 OUNCES FRESH BLOOD ORANGE JUICE (FROM APPROXIMATELY 10 BLOOD ORANGES), CHILLED

8 OUNCES VODKA, CHILLED

8 OUNCES MANDARINE NAPOLÉON LIQUEUR, CHILLED

1 BLOOD ORANGE, CUT INTO ¼-INCH SLICES, FOR GARNISH

GLASSWARE

PUNCH BOWL
AND PUNCH CUPS
(SEE PAGE 23)

PLANNING AHEAD
The punch should be served very cold, so either refrigerate all of the ingredients the night before you assemble the punch, or chill the prepared punch overnight.

Cut the pomegranate in half. Holding each half over a large bowl, squeeze firmly to extract the juice. Use a large spoon to scoop out as many seeds as possible and add them to the juice.

Be careful not to spray the seeds everywhere, as they can stain.

Transfer the pomegranate seeds and juice to the punch bowl. Add the blood orange juice, vodka, and Mandarine Napoléon and stir well to combine. Float the blood orange slices on top and serve.

WHISKEY AND GINGER PUNCH

Spicy ginger beer and bone-warming bourbon make this a great punch to serve in the late fall and winter when you need something to ward off the chill. It calls for Maker's Mark bourbon, for its sweetness, but feel free to substitute your favorite scotch, rye, or other bourbon.

ONE 3-INCH PIECE FRESH GINGER, PEELED AND CUT INTO ¼-INCH SLICES

½ CUP SUGAR

16 OUNCES MAKER'S MARK BOURBON, CHILLED

4 OUNCES FRESH LIME JUICE (FROM APPROXIMATELY 4 LIMES), CHILLED

FOUR 12-OUNCE BOTTLES GINGER BEER, CHILLED

2 LIMES, CUT INTO ¼-INCH ROUNDS

FRESHLY GRATED NUTMEG, FOR GARNISH

GLASSWARE

PUNCH BOWL AND PUNCH CUPS (SEE PAGE 23)

PLANNING AHEAD

The punch should be served very cold, so either refrigerate all of the ingredients the night before you assemble the punch or chill the prepared punch overnight, minus the ginger beer. Add the ginger beer before serving.

Place the ginger and sugar in the punch bowl and muddle (see page 18).

Add the bourbon and lime juice and stir. Let stand for 5 minutes.

Add the ginger beer and limes and stir well. Sprinkle nutmeg over the top and serve.

BANANA RUM PUNCH

MAKES TWENTY 5½-OUNCE SERVINGS

Even if you're sure you don't need the full twenty servings this recipe allows for, go ahead and make the full recipe of banana rum. It has a number of good uses (see Bonus from the Bar) and keeps indefinitely once the bananas are strained.

FOR THE BANANA RUM

12 DRIED BANANA SLICES OR
2 CUPS DRIED BANANA CHIPS

4 OUNCES BOILING WATER

2 OUNCES UNSULFURED MOLASSES

¼ CUP PACKED BROWN SUGAR

1 LITER DARK RUM

1 LARGE VANILLA BEAN

FOR THE PUNCH

4 LARGE RIPE, FRESH BANANAS,
PEELED AND FROZEN UNTIL FIRM

A HANDFUL OF DRIED BANANAS
OR BANANA CHIPS

16 OUNCES PINEAPPLE JUICE

1 LITER PEAR OR APPLE CIDER,
OR GINGER BEER

SHREDDED COCONUT, FOR GARNISH

GLASSWARE

A PITCHER AND GLASSES
(SEE PAGE 23)
or
A PUNCH BOWL
AND PUNCH CUPS
(SEE PAGE 23)

PLANNING AHEAD
The banana rum can be made as few as 4 hours in advance, but it is ideal after 48 hours.

To prepare the banana rum, cut the dried banana slices in half and place them in a large canning jar or pitcher with a tight-fitting lid. Add the water, molasses, and brown sugar, stir well, and let sit for 2 minutes. *continued*

Stir in the rum. Split the vanilla bean in half lengthwise and scrape out the seeds. Add the seeds and bean to the rum. Shake or stir vigorously to mix all ingredients. Refrigerate for up to 48 hours, stirring or shaking occasionally. After 48 hours at most, strain the rum, discarding the vanilla bean and reserving the bananas for another use (see Bonus from the Bar).

When ready to serve, place the frozen bananas in a pitcher or punch bowl and add the banana rum with the dried bananas or banana chips, pineapple juice, and cider or ginger beer.

Sprinkle shredded coconut over the top and serve.

✷ BONUS FROM THE BAR
The bananas that are strained out of the banana rum make a delicious topping for ice cream or cake. Also, once the pineapple juice is added, the cocktail mix itself (combined with some soy sauce) can be used as a marinade and base for grilled chicken or fish.

CHAPTER

-3-

BUBBLES

FROM THE LOUD POP of the cork to the gush of the first pour into the glass, sparkling wines and Champagnes always have a festive and celebratory feel to them. While most people think about serving sparkling wines for a special occasion, they are actually great food wines, perfect for brunch, lunch, or a dinner party. Their acidity and effervescence cut through rich foods and are a refreshing counterbalance to hot, spicy dishes. They also make interesting, decadent cocktails.

UNLESS OTHERWISE SPECIFIED, all the recipes in this book use a brut-style sparkling wine. Brut is one of the driest styles of sparkling wines and also the most widely available. All Champagnes are sparkling wines; not all sparkling wines, however, are Champagnes. Champagne is made only in the Champagne region of France, about sixty miles east of Paris. Any sparkling wine that does not come from this region is not true Champagne.

ASIDE FROM FRENCH Champagne, wonderful sparkling wines are being produced all over the world. For example, Prosecco, produced in Italy, and Cava, produced in Spain, are some other wonderful options for a quality sparkling wine.

CHERRY SUGAR FIZZ

MAKES FOUR 5½-OUNCE DRINKS

This cocktail may look as if it will be overly sweet, but it is well balanced by the bitters and the natural acidity of the sparkling wine. Contrary to my usual instructions for rimming a glass, this glass is dipped in syrup so that the sugar coating covers both the inside and outside of the rim, ensuring that with every sip, you get just enough cherry sugar flavor to balance the drink.

5 TEASPOONS SYRUP FROM
MARASCHINO CHERRIES,
FOR RIMMING THE GLASSES

¼ CUP GRANULATED SUGAR,
FOR RIMMING THE GLASSES

12 MARASCHINO CHERRIES

4 BROWN SUGAR CUBES

8 DASHES ANGOSTURA BITTERS

ONE 750-MILLILITER BOTTLE
SPARKLING WINE, CHILLED

GLASSWARE

4 CHAMPAGNE GLASSES
(SEE PAGE 20)

PLANNING AHEAD
Chill the sparkling wine for at least 30 minutes before making the cocktails.

Pour the cherry syrup onto a small plate and pour the sugar onto another. Working with one champagne glass at a time, invert it and dip the rim in the syrup, allowing any excess to drip off, then immediately dip lightly in the sugar. The sugar rim should be a light pink color.

Place 3 maraschino cherries, a brown sugar cube, and 2 dashes of bitters in each glass. Fill the glasses with the sparkling wine and serve immediately.

MAGNIFICENT MIMOSA

MAKES SIX 6-OUNCE DRINKS

The mimosa gets a bum rap and is too often served as a cheap add-on during a fixed-price brunch. The concoction of a not-so-great sparkling wine with too much orange juice has decimated the image of the mimosa. Using fresh-squeezed juice and Cointreau will give you a delightful beverage worthy of your holiday table. It makes a wonderful aperitif, or try serving it with a first course of smoked salmon or seared scallops. And unlike most still, dry wines, the mimosa will stand up to a strong vinaigrette in a salad course.

ONE 750-MILLILITER BOTTLE
SPARKLING WINE, CHILLED

12 OUNCES FRESH ORANGE JUICE
(FROM APPROXIMATELY 4 ORANGES)

3 OUNCES COINTREAU

GLASSWARE

6 CHAMPAGNE GLASSES
(SEE PAGE 20)

PLANNING AHEAD
*Chill the sparkling wine for at least
30 minutes before making the cocktails.*

Divide the sparkling wine evenly among the champagne glasses. This will work out to approximately 4 ounces per glass.

Top each glass with 2 ounces of orange juice, then float ½ ounce of Cointreau on top of each. Serve and sip slowly.

FRENCH 75

Named after a piece of French artillery used during World War I, this drink was originally made with gin. Over time it became more popular made with brandy. Try experimenting with both versions. Serve at a dressy soiree.

6 BROWN OR WHITE SUGAR CUBES OR 3 TEASPOONS GRANULATED BROWN OR WHITE SUGAR

12 DASHES ORANGE BITTERS

6 OUNCES GIN OR BRANDY

6 LEMON WEDGES

ONE 750-MILLILITER BOTTLE SPARKLING WINE, CHILLED

6 ORANGE TWISTS (SEE PAGE 66), FOR GARNISH (OPTIONAL)

GLASSWARE

6 CHAMPAGNE GLASSES (SEE PAGE 20; A COUPE IS SHOWN IN THE PHOTO OPPOSITE)

PLANNING AHEAD
Chill the sparkling wine for at least 30 minutes before making the cocktails.

In each of the champagne glasses, place 1 sugar cube or ½ teaspoon sugar, 2 dashes orange bitters, and 1 ounce gin.

Squeeze a lemon wedge into each glass and discard the wedge. Stir.

Divide the sparkling wine evenly among the glasses, garnish each with an orange twist, and serve.

BLOOD ORANGE SPARKLER

MAKES SIX 5-OUNCE DRINKS

Blood oranges are a seasonal treat; look for them from December to May. They are grown throughout the Mediterranean as well as in California.

1 BLOOD ORANGE

3 TEASPOONS SUGAR

3 TEASPOONS SWEET VERMOUTH

ONE 750-MILLILITER BOTTLE SPARKLING WINE, CHILLED

1 BLOOD ORANGE, CUT INTO ¼-INCH SLICES, FOR GARNISH

GLASSWARE

6 WINEGLASSES (SEE PAGE 20)

PLANNING AHEAD
Chill the sparkling wine for at least 30 minutes before making the cocktails.

Using a sharp knife, cut off and discard the ends of the blood orange. Stand it upright on a cutting board and slice the rind and white pith off the fruit using a gentle downward sawing motion, cutting away as little of the flesh as possible. Discard the rinds.

Cut the fruit crosswise into ½-inch slices. Divide the slices evenly among the wineglasses.

Sprinkle ½ teaspoon sugar into each glass and muddle to extract the orange juice (see page 18). Add ½ teaspoon vermouth to each glass and stir.

Divide the sparkling wine evenly among the glasses, stir, garnish each with a blood orange slice, and serve.

KIR ROYALE

A Kir is a classic French aperitif that combines crème de cassis, a liqueur made from black currants, with dry white wine. The Kir Royale is made with sparkling wine. It is worth paying more for a better brand of crème de cassis, as it makes an eminently better drink. Consider trying the delicious cassis made by Clinton Vineyards, in New York State.

ONE 750-MILLILITER BOTTLE
SPARKLING WINE, CHILLED

5 OUNCES CRÈME DE CASSIS

5 LONG LEMON SWIRLS FROM
APPROXIMATELY 2 LEMONS
(SEE SIDEBAR), FOR GARNISH

PLANNING AHEAD
*Chill the sparkling wine for at least
30 minutes before making the cocktails.*

GLASSWARE

5 CHAMPAGNE GLASSES
(SEE PAGE 20)

Divide the sparkling wine evenly among the champagne glasses and add 1 ounce cassis to each glass.

Garnish each glass with a lemon swirl, placing one end inside the drink and hanging the other end over the edge of the glass. Serve.

LEMON SWIRLS

Swirls are long strips of zest cut from the circumference of the fruit so they have a curly, springy look. You can use either a channel knife or a vegetable peeler to make them. Dig the curved blade of the knife or peeler into the skin of the fruit and pull it around the circumference (instead of from top to bottom).

PARK AVENUE

This intriguing blend of ingredients forms a unique cocktail that is perfect as a dinner preprandial. The Park Avenue is an acquired taste, but once it is acquired, one's taste for it never wanes. If you don't have leftover red wine to make the syrup, you can substitute grenadine, berry syrup, or simple syrup.

GRANULATED SUGAR, FOR RIMMING
THE GLASSES

1 LEMON WEDGE, FOR RIMMING
THE GLASSES

6 TEASPOONS RED WINE SYRUP
OR SIMPLE SYRUP
(PAGE 71)

6 OUNCES BRANDY

ONE 750-MILLILITER BOTTLE
SPARKLING WINE, CHILLED

3 OUNCES GRAND MARNIER

GLASSWARE

6 CHAMPAGNE GLASSES
(SEE PAGE 20)

PLANNING AHEAD
*Chill the sparkling wine for at least
30 minutes before making the cocktails.*

Pour the sugar onto a small plate. Rub the juicy side of the lemon wedge along the outer edge of the lip of each champagne glass—not along the inside of the rim. Holding each glass at an angle, roll the outer edge of the rim in the sugar until it is fully coated.

In each glass, place 1 teaspoon syrup and 1 ounce brandy. Stir well.

Divide the sparkling wine evenly among the glasses. Float ½ ounce Grand Marnier on top of each drink and serve.

THANKSGIVING SPARKLER

One Thanksgiving I went looking for a little something more to sip as the pumpkin pie was being served. I spied a half-filled bottle of Champagne, and inspiration struck. Sparkling wine is combined here with traditional Thanksgiving flavors for a festive drink that is a perfect accompaniment to hors d'oeuvres or dessert.

GRANULATED BROWN SUGAR, FOR RIMMING THE GLASSES

LEMON WEDGE, FOR RIMMING THE GLASSES

SCANT ⅛ TEASPOON GROUND CINNAMON

SCANT ⅛ TEASPOON GROUND CLOVES

SCANT ⅛ TEASPOON GROUND ALLSPICE

SCANT ⅛ TEASPOON GROUND GINGER

5 BROWN SUGAR CUBES

5 OUNCES BRANDY

ONE 750-MILLILITER BOTTLE SPARKLING WINE, CHILLED

FRESHLY GRATED NUTMEG, FOR GARNISH

GLASSWARE

5 CHAMPAGNE GLASSES (SEE PAGE 20)

PLANNING AHEAD
Chill the sparkling wine for at least 30 minutes before making the cocktails.

Pour the sugar onto a small plate. Rub the juicy side of the lemon wedge along the outer edge of the lip of each champagne glass—not along the inside of the rim. Holding each glass at an angle, roll the outer edge of the rim in the sugar until it is fully coated.

In a small bowl or ramekin, mix together the cinnamon, cloves, allspice, and ginger, then divide the mixture evenly among the glasses.

Add 1 sugar cube and 1 ounce brandy to each glass. Stir well until the spices are well blended into the brandy.

Divide the sparkling wine evenly among the glasses, sprinkle nutmeg on top, and serve.

BRANDYWINE SOUR

The flavor of the finished drink can vary quite dramatically—with undertones of almonds or orange blossoms or the predominant flavor of the dessert wine used.

ICE, FOR SERVING

8 OUNCES LEMON SOUR MIX
(RECIPE FOLLOWS)

4 OUNCES DESSERT WINE, CHILLED

8 OUNCES BRANDY

4 TEASPOONS RED WINE SYRUP
(PAGE 71)

GLASSWARE

4 ROCKS GLASSES
(SEE PAGE 19)

PLANNING AHEAD
Chill the wine for at least 30 minutes before making the cocktails.

Fill the rocks glasses with ice.

Fill a large pitcher with ice and add the sour mix, dessert wine, and brandy. Stir briskly until the mixture is frothy.

Strain the sour into the glasses. Float 1 teaspoon red wine syrup on top of each cocktail and serve.

Lemon or Lime Sour Mix

MAKES 6 CUPS MIX, ENOUGH FOR 12 TO 24 DRINKS,
DEPENDING ON THE COCKTAIL

Sour mix is called for in so many cocktails that it makes sense to prepare a quantity of it in advance to keep on hand. The egg whites make an ethereal, light cocktail with a layer of delicate foam and froth. Use fresh egg whites, or if you're concerned about using raw eggs, liquid or powdered pasteurized egg whites will work. This recipe halves or doubles perfectly.

1 QUART FRESHLY SQUEEZED
LEMON OR LIME JUICE
(FROM 24 TO 30 LEMONS OR LIMES)

1 CUP EGG WHITES, FROM
APPROXIMATELY 8 LARGE EGGS OR
6 TO 7 JUMBO EGGS

1 CUP SIMPLE SYRUP (PAGE 71),
OR MORE TO TASTE

PLANNING AHEAD
You can juice all the fruit in advance and freeze the juice in a tightly sealed container for up to one month. Transfer it to the refrigerator at least 24 hours before using. This mix itself can be made several days ahead.

Pour the juice through a fine-mesh strainer into a bowl. Using a rubber spatula, scrape the pulp through the strainer to ensure that you get every drop of juice. Discard the pulp.

Add the egg whites and simple syrup and whisk thoroughly.

Strain the mixture once more through a fine-mesh strainer into a container with a tight-fitting lid. Taste the mix. It should taste true to the fruit but with a hint of sweetness. If you prefer it sweeter, add more syrup. Cover and chill thoroughly before using.

PEAR, POIRE

Many domestic and imported pear liqueurs and pear brandies are available. Choose one that is rich and a little sweet as opposed to one that is sharp. One recommended brand is Belle de Brillet from France.

1 OUNCE FRESH LEMON JUICE
(FROM APPROXIMATELY 1 LEMON)

2 TEASPOONS SUGAR

1 SMALL RIPE BARTLETT PEAR

6 OUNCES PEAR LIQUEUR

ONE 750-MILLILITER BOTTLE
SPARKLING WINE, CHILLED

GLASSWARE

6 CHAMPAGNE GLASSES
(SEE PAGE 20)

PLANNING AHEAD
You can prepare the diced pears up to 8 hours in advance and store them in the refrigerator. Chill the sparkling wine for at least 30 minutes before making the cocktails.

Place the lemon juice and sugar in a bowl and stir to combine.

Peel, core, and chop the pear into ¼-inch dice and add it to the bowl. Add the pear liqueur and stir well.

Divide the pear mixture evenly among the champagne glasses. Fill each glass with the sparkling wine and serve.

CHAPTER
-4-

CLASSIC COCKTAILS & A TWIST

JUST WHAT MAKES A COCKTAIL a classic? The *American Heritage Dictionary* lists several definitions of *classic*, including "of the highest rank or class," "serving as the established model or standard," and "having lasting historical, cultural, or literary associations." Combine these three definitions and you get a sense of what a classic cocktail is.

CLASSIC COCKTAILS ALSO lead to inspiration. They encourage us to create new tastes, textures, and approaches to the standards. From these classics, basic techniques are learned and mastered and an exponential number of new cocktails are invented. The drinks in this chapter are those I turn to again and again. They are all perfect for entertaining and, I hope, will tempt you to take the next step of creating your own signature cocktails.

MANHATTAN

The original Manhattan, created in 1874 at the Manhattan Club in New York, was made with sweet vermouth and rye, which produces a smooth, mellow cocktail. Over time, multiple variations of the Manhattan have developed, with tweaks to both the whiskey and the vermouth, so that today you have a classic sweet Manhattan, made with sweet vermouth; a Dry Manhattan (page 66), made with dry vermouth; and a Perfect Manhattan (page 67), made with equal amounts of both. No matter what style you prefer, don't be afraid to use the bitters, as they make the drink fuller and more flavorful.

4½ OUNCES RYE OR
BOURBON WHISKEY

1½ OUNCES SWEET VERMOUTH

2 DASHES ANGOSTURA BITTERS

2 MARASCHINO CHERRIES,
FOR GARNISH

GLASSWARE

2 COCKTAIL GLASSES
(SEE PAGE 20)

Fill a 1-quart pitcher with ice and add the whiskey, sweet vermouth, and bitters. Stir vigorously until the outside of the pitcher is thoroughly beaded with sweat and is extremely cold to the touch.

Place a maraschino cherry in each cocktail glass. Strain the drink over the cherries and serve immediately.

DRY MANHATTAN

Dry Manhattans make a great palate opener before dinner. Substituting Lillet Blanc for the vermouth adds a distinctive orange note and more fruitiness. Also, try using an orange twist instead of lemon.

4½ OUNCES RYE OR
BOURBON WHISKEY

1½ OUNCES DRY VERMOUTH OR
LILLET BLANC

2 DASHES ANGOSTURA BITTERS

2 LEMON TWISTS (SEE SIDEBAR),
FOR GARNISH

GLASSWARE

2 COCKTAIL GLASSES
(SEE PAGE 20)

Fill a 1-quart pitcher with ice and add the whiskey, dry vermouth, and bitters. Stir vigorously until the outside of the pitcher is thoroughly beaded with sweat and is extremely cold to the touch.

Strain into the cocktail glasses, then twist the lemon over each drink and drop it in. Serve immediately.

LEMON OR ORANGE TWISTS

Twists are 1- to 2-inch-long oval or rectangular slivers of lemon or other citrus rind that are twisted over a cocktail, releasing their essential oils into the drink.

To make them, start by cutting off the "polar" nubs at each end of the fruit. Then place the fruit on one flat end and use a paring knife to gently cut off a slice of the rind, starting at the top and working your way downward. Try not to get too much of the bitter white pith. Alternatively, you can use a vegetable peeler. Hold the fruit firmly in the palm of your hand. Starting at one end and cutting straight toward the other end, carefully and steadily remove a slice of the rind.

PERFECT MANHATTAN

Adding both sweet and dry vermouth makes the Perfect Manhattan a complex marriage of flavors. For a truly unique drink, substitute cherry brandy for the sweet vermouth. The result is a dry fruit flavor that is both refreshing and palate cleansing.

4½ OUNCES RYE OR
BOURBON WHISKEY

¾ OUNCE DRY VERMOUTH

¾ OUNCE SWEET VERMOUTH OR
CHERRY BRANDY

2 DASHES ANGOSTURA BITTERS

2 LEMON TWISTS (SEE PAGE 66),
FOR GARNISH

GLASSWARE

2 COCKTAIL GLASSES
(SEE PAGE 20)

Fill a 1-quart pitcher with ice and add the whiskey, dry vermouth, sweet vermouth, and bitters. Stir vigorously until the outside of the pitcher is thoroughly beaded with sweat and is extremely cold to the touch.

Strain the drink into the cocktail glasses, twist the lemon over the drink, and drop it in. Serve immediately.

OLD-FASHIONED

The great thing about the old-fashioned is that it can easily be made more or less sweet or more or less diluted, as you prefer, without impinging on the integrity of the drink.

2 HALF SLICES OF ORANGE, FOR MUDDLING

2 MARASCHINO CHERRIES

1 TEASPOON SUGAR

ICE, FOR SERVING

6 OUNCES BOURBON, RYE, SCOTCH, OR BRANDY

4 OUNCES CLUB SODA

GLASSWARE

2 ROCKS GLASSES (SEE PAGE 19)

Place 1 orange half slice, 1 cherry, and ⅓ teaspoon sugar in each rocks glass. Muddle until the fruit is well mashed and mixed with the sugar (see page 18).

Fill the glasses with ice, add the bourbon, and stir well. Top off with soda, stir, and serve.

MINT JULEP

Juleps inspire many arguments about the *correct* way to make them and, of course, whether it was Virginians or Kentuckians who created them. Regardless of the answer to these worthy debates, the julep remains a lovely predinner drink.

6 FRESH MINT SPRIGS

1 OUNCE SIMPLE SYRUP (RECIPE FOLLOWS) OR 2 TEASPOONS SUGAR

CRUSHED ICE, FOR SERVING

4 OUNCES BOURBON

GLASSWARE

2 ROCKS GLASSES (SEE PAGE 19), CHILLED
or
2 SILVER JULEP CUPS, CHILLED

PLANNING AHEAD
Place the glasses in the freezer or refrigerator 20 minutes before making the drinks.

Place 2 mint sprigs and ½ ounce simple syrup in the bottom of each rocks glass or julep cup. Muddle well (see page 18).

Fill the glasses or cups with crushed ice and add the bourbon. Stir well, until the glasses or cups are frosted. Garnish with the remaining mint and serve.

Simple Syrup

Simple syrup allows sugar, which has been heated in water and dissolved, to blend more easily than granulated sugar into iced tea, coffee, and lemonade. Syrups may also "float" on top of a cocktail (see page 18 for the proper floating technique). Since the syrups last a couple of weeks in the refrigerator, you can use part of a batch and save the rest for later.

This recipe for plain sugar syrup provides the template for the variations that follow.

2 CUPS SUGAR

1 CUP WATER

PLANNING AHEAD
Simple syrup can be made up to 2 weeks in advance and stored in a very clean container in the refrigerator.

Place the sugar and water in a small saucepan and stir to combine. Bring to a gentle boil over medium-high heat. Reduce the heat and simmer until the sugar is completely dissolved and the syrup is slightly thickened, about 3 minutes.

Remove from the heat and let cool. Transfer the syrup to a container with a tight-fitting lid, cover, and refrigerate until ready to use.

VARIATIONS
....

Brown Sugar Syrup: Substitute brown sugar for regular sugar.

Red Wine Syrup: This variation can be made up to 3 weeks in advance and yields 3 cups of syrup. Substitute 2 cups of red wine for the 1 cup of water, and increase the sugar to 2 cups. Simmer for 15 minutes instead of 3 minutes.

PEAR COBBLER

MAKES TWO 5-OUNCE DRINKS

This drink is based on the classic sidecar, a sublime mixture of fresh lemon juice, brandy, and Cointreau. The pear cobbler replaces the brandy with pear liqueur while the lemon and orange flavors remain the same, resulting in a delightfully crisp and fruity fall drink. If you can't find pear liqueur (Belle de Brillet is a good choice), replace it with 4 ounces brandy and 2 ounces pear nectar; this will yield two 6-ounce cocktails.

Try serving the Pear Cobbler with biscotti or shortbread cookies and dried fruit for a light dessert.

4 OUNCES LEMON SOUR MIX (PAGE 60)

4 OUNCES PEAR LIQUEUR

2 OUNCES TRIPLE SEC

2 DRIED PEAR SLICES, FOR GARNISH

GLASSWARE

2 COCKTAIL GLASSES (SEE PAGE 20), CHILLED

Fill a cocktail shaker or pitcher with ice. Add the sour mix and shake or stir vigorously.

Add the pear liqueur and triple sec. Shake or stir until the mix appears frothy on top.

Pour into the chilled cocktail glasses. Float a dried pear slice on top of each drink and serve immediately.

APPLE CRUSH

MAKES FOUR 5-OUNCE DRINKS

This drink was inspired by a holiday pie-making marathon. Rome apples' texture and acidity are perfectly balanced; they have a creamy feel in your mouth yet enough structure to stand up well to cooking. Use your own favorite here, and whether they are tart and very firm or sweet and slightly soft to the bite, make sure to buy fresh, local apples in season. Calvados, a French apple brandy, fortifies the flavor in this recipe.

1 ROME APPLE

3 OUNCES FRESH LEMON JUICE (FROM APPROXIMATELY 2 LEMONS), LEMON RINDS RESERVED

2 TABLESPOONS MAPLE SUGAR OR 2 TEASPOONS GROUND CINNAMON MIXED WITH 4 TEASPOONS SUGAR, FOR RIMMING THE GLASSES

10 OUNCES CALVADOS OR APPLEJACK

4 OUNCES VODKA

4 OUNCES FRESH-PRESSED APPLE CIDER

GLASSWARE

4 COCKTAIL GLASSES (SEE PAGE 20)

PLANNING AHEAD

The apple must be chilled for at least 15 minutes and can be refrigerated for up to 1 hour.

Peel, core, and dice the apple into ½-inch cubes. Place the apple in a zippered plastic bag and add about 1 tablespoon of the lemon juice. Seal the bag and toss gently (this will help prevent discoloration). Chill thoroughly for 30 minutes in the refrigerator (the apple can stay in the refrigerator for up to 1 hour) or 15 minutes in the freezer.

When ready to serve, pour the maple sugar onto a small plate. Rub the juicy side of the reserved lemon rind (cut the rind if necessary to expose this side) along the outer edge of the lip of each glass—not along the inside of the rim. Holding each glass at an angle, roll the outer edge of the rim in the sugar until it is fully coated.

Fill a cocktail shaker with ice and add the calvados, vodka, cider, and remaining lemon juice.

Shake vigorously until the outside of the shaker is thoroughly beaded with sweat and is extremely cold to the touch. Divide the apple cubes evenly among the cocktail glasses, pour the drink over them, and serve.

ROSMARINO

This savory cocktail's unique and spirited taste comes from rosemary-infused vodka. The addition of vermouth and Pernod, an anise-based liqueur, makes this a potent and powerfully flavored cocktail, perfect to serve as an aperitif before a hearty holiday meal.

FOR THE ROSEMARY-INFUSED VODKA

FOUR 8-INCH BRANCHES
OF ROSEMARY, RINSED

2 OUNCES BOILING WATER

8 OUNCES ICE-COLD WATER

1 LITER VODKA

4 OUNCES DRY VERMOUTH

2 OUNCES PERNOD

FOR EACH 3-OUNCE COCKTAIL

2 BRINED CAPER BERRIES
(NOT SALTED), FOR GARNISH

GLASSWARE

COCKTAIL GLASSES
(SEE PAGE 20)

To prepare the rosemary-infused vodka, place the rosemary in a 2-quart canning jar or other container with a tight-fitting lid. Add the boiling water, close the jar tightly, and shake vigorously. Allow to steep until the rosemary is bright green, about 10 minutes.

Open the jar and add the ice water, vodka, vermouth, and Pernod. Close the jar tightly and shake vigorously. Allow to steep in a cool spot or the refrigerator for 2 days, until the liquid turns bright green. Remove and discard the rosemary.

Place two caper berries in the bottom of each cocktail glass.

Fill a cocktail shaker with ice, add 3 ounces of rosemary-infused vodka per serving, and shake vigorously until the outside of the shaker is thoroughly beaded with sweat and is extremely cold to the touch.

Pour the vodka over the caper berries and serve.

GRAPE AND GRAIN

I first made this straightforward variation of the Old-Fashioned (page 68) one autumn when cherries were out of season but fat, ripe grapes were just coming in. Use the darkest grapes you can find, as they generally have the richest flavor. Don't worry about seeds; they won't hurt the drink. For a stronger bourbon taste, use less seltzer.

16 BLACK GRAPES

4 HALF SLICES OF ORANGE

4 TEASPOONS SUGAR

8 DASHES ANGOSTURA BITTERS

ICE, FOR SERVING

12 OUNCES BOURBON

12 OUNCES SELTZER

GLASSWARE

4 ROCKS GLASSES
(SEE PAGE 19)

Place 4 grapes in each rocks glass along with 1 orange half slice, 1 teaspoon sugar, and 2 dashes bitters. Muddle the ingredients together (see page 18).

Fill the glasses with ice. Add 3 ounces bourbon to each glass and stir well. Top off each glass with seltzer and serve.

MARASCHINO MUDDLE

-nonalcoholic-

MAKES SIX 4-OUNCE DRINKS

I was making Old-Fashioneds (page 68) one evening when I noticed that a pregnant friend was eating my whole batch of maraschino cherries. I made her this drink in the interest of saving my stock of cherries. The beverage has a winelike flavor and complexity, so I heartily recommend serving it with dinner as well as for an aperitif.

8 OUNCES FRESH LEMON JUICE
(FROM 5 TO 6 LEMONS)

8 OUNCES FRESH LIME JUICE
(FROM APPROXIMATELY 8 LIMES)

4 OUNCES NATURAL WHITE
GRAPE JUICE

1 OUNCE ORANGE FLOWER WATER

12 MARASCHINO CHERRIES

2 OUNCES SYRUP FROM
MARASCHINO CHERRIES

3 TEASPOONS SUGAR

6 DASHES PEYCHAUD'S BITTERS

6 HALF SLICES OF ORANGE

ICE, FOR SERVING

CLUB SODA

GLASSWARE

4 ROCKS GLASSES
(SEE PAGE 19)

Fill a cocktail shaker or tall pitcher with ice and add the lemon and lime juices, grape juice, and orange flower water. Shake or stir vigorously.

In each rocks glass, place 2 maraschino cherries, ⅓ ounce cherry syrup, ½ teaspoon sugar, a dash of bitters, and a half orange slice. Muddle thoroughly (see page 18).

Fill each glass with ice and pour in the juice mixture. Stir vigorously until well blended. Top off with club soda and serve.

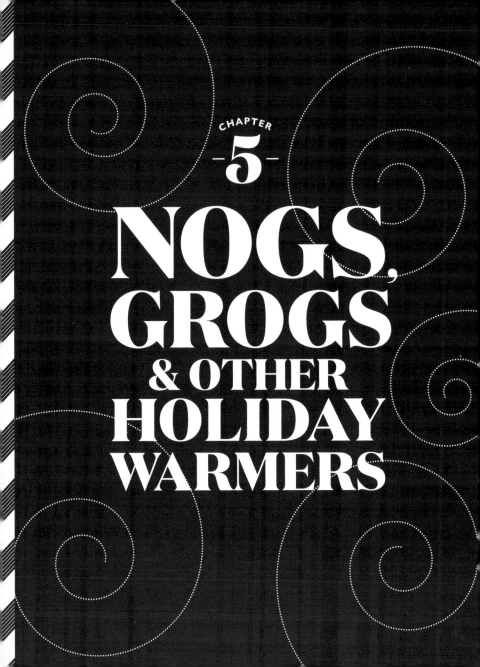

CHAPTER

-5-

NOGS, GROGS

& OTHER HOLIDAY WARMERS

NOTHING BEATS THE COLD like a piping hot drink, no matter how old you are. Nogs can be served warm or cold and are made with a base of cream or eggs. They are always rich, thick, and decadent. Grogs were originally made from rum, sugar, molasses, lemon, and water and could be served either hot or cold. Over time, the term *grog* has come to refer to a hot beverage with rum.

THE FOLLOWING RECIPES are hearty mugs of potent potables—nogs and grogs meant to warm both body and spirit and maybe even rekindle our youth for a few moments. Serve these winter warmers right after a day of cold-weather play, for dessert, or as a nightcap.

IF YOU'RE LOOKING for other favorite hot drinks such as toddies and spiced coffee, you'll find them later in the book in "After-Dinner Drinks"; they're so good they deserve their own chapter.

HOLIDAY EGGNOG

Though many eggnogs use raw eggs, this one is based on classic crème anglaise, so the eggs are cooked. After you make this base, the variety of liquor, the spices, and the consistency are up to you. I like my eggnog rich, thick, and spicy. For a nonalcoholic version, simply eliminate the liquor and add a little more milk or cream to get the desired consistency.

FOR THE CRÈME ANGLAISE

16 OUNCES MILK

4 LARGE EGG YOLKS

3 TABLESPOONS SUGAR

2 TABLESPOONS FLOUR

PINCH OF SALT

1 TEASPOON VANILLA EXTRACT

FOR THE NOG

16 OUNCES MILK

16 OUNCES HEAVY CREAM

¼ TEASPOON GROUND CINNAMON

⅛ TEASPOON GROUND CLOVES

6 OUNCES DARK RUM

3 OUNCES BOURBON

3 OUNCES BRANDY

PLANNING AHEAD
The nog can be made up to 12 hours in advance and stored in the refrigerator. Just give it a good whisking before serving.

½ CUP CONFECTIONERS' SUGAR (OPTIONAL)

FRESHLY GRATED NUTMEG, FOR GARNISH

GRATED ORANGE ZEST, FOR GARNISH (OPTIONAL)

GLASSWARE

PUNCH BOWL AND PUNCH CUPS (SEE PAGE 23)

continued

To prepare the crème anglaise, have ready a large bowl full of ice. You'll also need a double boiler. (Instead, you can use a medium-large saucepan and a heatproof bowl that fits in the saucepan without touching the bottom and whose edges hang over the edges of the saucepan.)

Place the milk in a saucepan over high heat. As soon as it begins to boil, stir briskly and remove from the heat. Meanwhile, in the bottom of the double boiler, add just enough water so that the top half of the double boiler does not touch the water. Bring to a boil, then reduce to a low simmer.

In the top of the double boiler, whisk together the egg yolks, sugar, flour, and salt. Whisking constantly, slowly pour in the hot milk.

Cook the mixture over, not in, the simmering water, stirring constantly until the mixture is thickened and coats the back of a spoon.

Remove the double boiler top from the heat and set it in the bowl of ice for 5 minutes, stirring the mixture occasionally. Add the vanilla and stir.

To prepare the eggnog, in a large bowl, combine the crème anglaise with the milk, cream, cinnamon, cloves, rum, bourbon, and brandy. Taste, adding as much confectioners' sugar as you wish for a sweeter nog.

Transfer the eggnog to the punch bowl and sprinkle nutmeg and orange zest over it, if desired. Chill for an hour or serve at room temperature.

THANKSGIVING NOG

MAKES SIX 7½-OUNCE SERVINGS

The inspiration for this nog was the roasted pumpkin left over from pumpkin soup. Serve this drink warm after dinner with a big plate of cookies.

8 OUNCES WATER

8 OUNCES MILK OR CREAM

½ CUP DARK BROWN SUGAR

1 TABLESPOON MOLASSES

1 TEASPOON VANILLA

¼ TEASPOON GROUND CINNAMON, PLUS MORE FOR GARNISH

⅛ TEASPOON GROUND CLOVES

⅛ TEASPOON GROUND ALLSPICE

⅛ TEASPOON GROUND NUTMEG

⅛ TEASPOON GROUND MACE

ONE 15-OUNCE CAN (ABOUT 2 CUPS) PUMPKIN PUREE

10 OUNCES DARK RUM, BRANDY, OR BOURBON

WHIPPED CREAM, FOR GARNISH

6 CINNAMON STICKS, FOR GARNISH

GLASSWARE

6 IRISH COFFEE MUGS (SEE PAGE 23)
or
SEE TRICK OF THE TRADE

PLANNING AHEAD
The nog can be made a day or two in advance and refrigerated, then warmed on the stove or in the microwave when ready to serve. It can also be frozen for several weeks.

Stir together the water, milk, sugar, molasses, vanilla, and spices in a medium-large saucepan. Simmer on low heat, stirring regularly, until the sugar has dissolved and the spices are incorporated, about 5 minutes.

continued

Stir in the pumpkin and continue simmering until the nog is hot, about 15 minutes. It should be the consistency of very thick cream. If it seems too thick or pasty, add more water or milk. Bear in mind that the rum will thin the mixture further.

Remove the nog from the heat and stir in the rum. Ladle into the mugs, garnish with whipped cream, cinnamon sticks, and ground cinnamon, and serve.

TRICK OF THE TRADE

For an impressive holiday presentation, hollow out a large pumpkin and serve this drink in a pumpkin terrine. Or hollow out several small pumpkins and serve the nog in pumpkin "mugs."

IRIS'S COFFEE NOG

MAKES SIXTEEN 4-OUNCE SERVINGS

Modesto Battista, the chief steward of Gramercy Tavern, oversees anything and everything. On a few cold and lucky Saturday mornings, his wife, Iris, made a nonalcoholic version of this nog for the staff. Modesto would thump his chest and say that it makes you strong, and I believe him. Here is the spiked version. Try serving this as dessert at Sunday brunch. For a thicker nog, simmer it longer. If you prefer it thinner, add more coffee or milk.

FOR THE CRÈME ANGLAISE

16 OUNCES MILK

4 LARGE EGG YOLKS

3 TABLESPOONS SUGAR

2 TABLESPOONS FLOUR

PINCH OF SALT

1 TEASPOON VANILLA EXTRACT

PLANNING AHEAD
The nog can be made up to 12 hours in advance and stored in the refrigerator. Just give it a good whisking before serving.

FOR THE NOG

16 OUNCES STRONG BLACK COFFEE, AT ROOM TEMPERATURE

8 OUNCES MILK

8 OUNCES HEAVY CREAM

6 OUNCES DARK RUM

3 OUNCES KAHLÚA

½ CUP SUGAR

¼ TEASPOON GROUND CINNAMON

⅛ TEASPOON GROUND CLOVES

FRESHLY GRATED NUTMEG, FOR GARNISH

GLASSWARE

16 IRISH COFFEE MUGS (SEE PAGE 23)

To prepare the crème anglaise, have ready a large bowl full of ice and a double boiler. (Instead, you can use a medium-large saucepan with a heatproof bowl that fits in the saucepan without touching the bottom and whose edges hang over the edges of the saucepan.)

Place the milk in a saucepan over high heat. As soon as it begins to boil, stir briskly and remove from the heat. Meanwhile, in the bottom of the double boiler, add just enough water so that the top half of the double boiler does not touch the water. Bring to a boil, then reduce to a low simmer.

In the top of the double boiler, whisk together the egg yolks, sugar, flour, and salt. Whisking constantly, slowly pour in the hot milk.

Cook the mixture over, not in, the simmering water, stirring constantly until the mixture is thickened and coats the back of a spoon.

Remove the double boiler top from the heat and set in the bowl of ice for 5 minutes, stirring occasionally. Add the vanilla and stir.

To prepare the nog, place the coffee, milk, cream, rum, Kahlúa, sugar, cinnamon, and cloves in a large saucepan over low heat. Heat just until the mixture is well blended and warm.

Add the crème anglaise and stir well to blend. Heat to the desired temperature.

Ladle into the mugs, sprinkle nutmeg on top, and serve.

GENERAL WASHINGTON'S GROG

MAKES FOUR 8-OUNCE SERVINGS

Many historical accounts reveal that General Washington loved to imbibe and even made his own whiskey at Mount Vernon. How else could you get through winters in Valley Forge? Rich and aromatic with warm spices, this grog is my ode to George. It is likely very similar to what the great general himself drank.

20 OUNCES WATER

4 OUNCES MADEIRA

4 OUNCES RUM

4 OUNCES BOURBON

4 TEASPOONS BROWN SUGAR

4 WHOLE CLOVES

4 CINNAMON STICKS

4 TABLESPOONS BUTTER (OPTIONAL)

GLASSWARE

4 IRISH COFFEE MUGS
(SEE PAGE 23)

In a medium saucepan, bring the water to a boil. Reduce the heat to a simmer and stir in the Madeira, rum, bourbon, brown sugar, cloves, and cinnamon sticks.

When the grog is hot, remove it from the heat. Using a slotted spoon, remove the cloves and cinnamon sticks; reserve the cinnamon sticks. Ladle the grog into the mugs, adding 1 reserved cinnamon stick to each. Float a tablespoon of butter on top of each, if desired, and serve.

BANANA BUTTERED RUM

MAKES TEN 8-OUNCE SERVINGS AND
ENOUGH BANANA BUTTER FOR 16 SERVINGS

Hot buttered rum is the quintessential winter drink, served in ski lodges across the world, where chilly skiers gladly warm their hands around steaming mugs. I often serve this banana-flavored toddy for dessert with a plate of butter cookies. I urge you to make the full batch of banana butter; whatever you don't use will last for several months and can be spread on warm pancakes or French toast. It even makes toasted store-bought raisin bread an especially yummy treat.

FOR THE BANANA BUTTER

1 POUND (4 STICKS) UNSALTED BUTTER, SOFTENED

1 RIPE BANANA, MASHED

½ POUND BROWN SUGAR

½ TABLESPOON GROUND CINNAMON

¼ TEASPOON FRESHLY GRATED NUTMEG

¼ TEASPOON GROUND CLOVES

FOR EACH SERVING

2 HEAPING TABLESPOONS BANANA BUTTER

2 OUNCES DARK RUM

BOILING WATER

1 OR 2 WHOLE STAR ANISE, FOR GARNISH

1 CINNAMON STICK, FOR GARNISH

GLASSWARE

10 IRISH COFFEE MUGS (SEE PAGE 23)

PLANNING AHEAD

The banana butter can be refrigerated for up to 1 week or frozen for up to 3 months. Let it come to room temperature before using. If it's frozen, thaw at room temperature or slice the frozen butter into 1-inch-thick pieces, arrange on a plate, and soften in the microwave for 10 seconds.

continued

To make the banana butter, place the butter, banana, brown sugar, cinnamon, nutmeg, and cloves in the bowl of a food processor and process until well combined. Roll the mixture into a cylinder in a piece of plastic wrap and refrigerate until ready to use. Let the butter come to room temperature before serving.

When ready to serve, add 2 heaping tablespoons banana butter to each mug. Top with 2 ounces rum and fill the mug two-thirds full with boiling water.

Float a star anise or two on top of the drink. Add a cinnamon stick and stir the mixture using the stick. Serve immediately.

VARIATION

Buttered Rum: Prepare the banana butter, above, omitting the banana and keeping all other ingredients as specified.

PUMPKIN CIDER

Many chefs add apples to their pumpkin soup to give it a hint of natural sweetness and complexity. Here, I have reversed the technique: The pumpkin lends a savory note to the sweet cider.

1 TABLESPOON BUTTER

1 TABLESPOON SUGAR

TWELVE 1-INCH CUBES PUMPKIN OR BUTTERNUT SQUASH

64 OUNCES FRESH APPLE CIDER

12 WHOLE CLOVES

6 WHOLE STAR ANISE

3 CINNAMON STICKS

12 OUNCES DARK RUM

12 OUNCES CALVADOS OR APPLEJACK

FRESHLY GRATED NUTMEG, FOR GARNISH

GLASSWARE

12 COFFEE CUPS
or
12 IRISH COFFEE MUGS
(SEE PAGE 23)

Preheat a large saucepan over medium heat. Add the butter, sugar, and pumpkin. Sauté the pumpkin, turning it regularly, until the sides have become slightly caramelized, about 8 minutes. If you feel the pumpkin becoming soft, remove the pan from the heat to avoid overcooking.

Stir in the cider, cloves, star anise, and cinnamon sticks. Reduce the heat to a simmer and cook, stirring regularly, until hot.

Remove the cinnamon sticks. Stir in the rum and calvados. Ladle into coffee cups or mugs, sprinkle nutmeg on top, and serve.

HOT SPIKED CIDER

MAKES EIGHT 11-OUNCE SERVINGS

Soaking the dried apples in calvados or applejack adds a kick to this smooth, mellow rum drink.

FOR THE DRUNKEN FRUIT

8 LARGE DRIED APPLE RINGS

SMALL HANDFUL OF DRIED CURRANTS (OPTIONAL)

4 OUNCES CALVADOS OR APPLEJACK

FOR THE DRINK

64 OUNCES FRESH APPLE CIDER

12 WHOLE CLOVES

6 WHOLE STAR ANISE

3 CINNAMON STICKS

½ TEASPOON FRESHLY GRATED NUTMEG

2 TABLESPOONS BROWN SUGAR, FOR DREDGING THE APPLE SLICES

24 OUNCES DARK RUM

8 EXTRA-LONG CINNAMON STICKS

GLASSWARE

8 IRISH COFFEE MUGS (SEE PAGE 23)

Place the dried apples and the currants, if using, in a large zippered plastic bag, add the calvados, and seal the bag. Allow to steep in the refrigerator overnight.

When ready to serve, gently warm the cider and spices in a pot—do not allow the mixture to boil. Meanwhile, remove the apple slices from the plastic bag and dredge each in the brown sugar.

Pour a healthy shot of rum into each mug and add the cider. (I don't mind if the mulling spices get into the finished drink, but if you prefer your drink without the spices, you can pour the cider through a fine-mesh strainer into the mugs.) Float a sugared apple slice on top of each drink, spoon the currants over the apples, add a cinnamon stick, and serve.

FIG MULLED WINE

MAKES 8 SERVINGS

This recipe is extremely versatile and can easily be doubled. Any leftover mulled wine can be kept in the refrigerator for up to four days. If you are not a fan of figs, use your favorite dried fruit, such as plums or cherries, instead. I often serve mulled wine in a soup terrine and allow my guests to serve themselves.

I usually use a California pinot noir because of its bright fruit, but any hearty wine with good fruit and low acid will be fine.

FOR THE FIG BASE

2 DOZEN DRIED BLACK MISSION FIGS

1 ORANGE

16 OUNCES PORT

½ CUP BROWN SUGAR

6 WHOLE CLOVES

4 TO 6 WHOLE STAR ANISE

3 CINNAMON STICKS

½ TEASPOON FRESHLY GRATED NUTMEG

FOR THE MULLED WINE

ONE 750-MILLILITER BOTTLE PINOT NOIR

8 OUNCES CHERRY BRANDY OR ANY DARK FRUIT BRANDY OR GRAND MARNIER

8 CINNAMON STICKS, FOR GARNISH

GLASSWARE

8 IRISH COFFEE MUGS (SEE PAGE 23) *and* A SOUP TERRINE, IF DESIRED

To prepare the fruit, trim the stems from the dried figs and discard. Cut the figs into small dice. Peel the rind from the orange and set aside. Cut the orange lengthwise into 8 segments, trimming and discarding any white pith.

To prepare the fig base, place the figs, orange segments, port, brown sugar, cloves, star anise, cinnamon sticks, and nutmeg in a large heavy-bottomed pot. Bring the mixture just to a boil over medium heat. Immediately reduce the heat to medium-low and simmer until the figs are extremely soft and the mixture is reduced almost to a glaze, 20 to 30 minutes.

Meanwhile, trim and discard the white pith from the reserved orange rind. Very thinly slice the rind and set it aside.

When the base is reduced, add the wine and brandy and simmer just until hot. Do not allow the mixture to boil. Discard the whole cloves, star anise, and cinnamon sticks.

Ladle the mulled wine into the mugs. Add a cinnamon stick and a bit of sliced orange rind to each mug and serve. Alternatively, pour all the mulled wine into a soup terrine, arrange the garnishes in the mugs, and let your guests serve themselves.

TRICK OF THE TRADE
For a steeped version of this drink, make the fig base and let it cool completely. Add the wine and brandy and refrigerate for up to 2 weeks, allowing the flavors to blend. When ready to serve, heat the mixture on the stovetop over low heat or "steam" individual servings in the microwave or with a cappuccino maker.

✳ BONUS FROM THE BAR
Fig Wine Topping: For a heavenly topping for ice cream or pound cake, simmer any remaining mulled wine over low heat in a heavy-bottomed pot until it reduces to a syrupy glaze, about 15 minutes, depending on the amount of liquid to be reduced. Let cool slightly before using as a topping.

APRICOT MULLED WINE

MAKES 8 SERVINGS

Though mulled wines are typically red, the urge to tinker with the classic led to this delicious variation. Riesling, with its peach and apricot notes, is a favorite wine variety because of its versatility, food friendliness, and incredible fruit flavors. You can substitute twelve dried peaches for the twenty-four dried apricots, if desired. If you want to make this recipe in advance, see the Trick of the Trade in Fig Mulled Wine (page 101) for heating and serving instructions.

A fun way to serve this is in a punch bowl—just be sure the bowl is heatproof. Add the cinnamon stick and orange rind garnishes directly to the punch bowl and, for an extra festive touch, peel and slice one or two oranges or blood oranges as for the Blood Orange Sparkler (page 52) and float the fruit slices on top.

FOR THE APRICOT BASE

1 ORANGE OR BLOOD ORANGE

24 DRIED APRICOTS, FINELY DICED

16 OUNCES APRICOT OR PEACH BRANDY

½ CUP SUGAR

6 WHOLE CLOVES

4 TO 6 WHOLE STAR ANISE

3 CINNAMON STICKS

½ TEASPOON FRESHLY GRATED NUTMEG

FOR THE MULLED WINE

ONE 750-MILLILITER BOTTLE RIESLING

8 OUNCES APRICOT OR PEACH BRANDY

8 CINNAMON STICKS

GLASSWARE

8 IRISH COFFEE MUGS (SEE PAGE 23)

continued

To prepare the apricot base, peel the rind from the orange and set it aside. Cut the orange lengthwise into 8 segments, trimming and discarding any white pith.

Place the orange segments, apricots, brandy, sugar, cloves, star anise, cinnamon sticks, and nutmeg in a large heavy-bottomed pot. Set over medium heat and bring the mixture just to a boil. Immediately reduce the heat to medium low and simmer, stirring often, until the apricots are extremely soft and the mixture is reduced almost to a glaze, 20 to 30 minutes.

Meanwhile, trim and discard the white pith from the reserved orange rind. Very thinly slice the rind and set aside.

When the base is reduced, add the wine and brandy and simmer just until hot. Do not allow the mixture to boil. Discard the whole cloves, star anise, and cinnamon sticks.

To serve, ladle the mulled wine into the mugs. Add a cinnamon stick and a bit of sliced orange rind to each mug and serve.

CHESTNUT
HOT CHOCOLATE

MAKES EIGHT 6-OUNCE SERVINGS

There used to be a store in Manhattan called Paprika Weiss that sold amazing chestnut puree dipped in chocolate; here it is in a mug. You can make this drink nonalcoholic by omitting the Frangelico and brandy.

24 OUNCES MILK

½ CUP SUGAR

PINCH OF GROUND CINNAMON

PINCH OF SALT

12 OUNCES DARK CHOCOLATE, CHOPPED INTO SMALL PIECES

12 OUNCES CHESTNUT PUREE

4 OUNCES FRANGELICO (OPTIONAL)

4 OUNCES BRANDY (OPTIONAL)

WHIPPED CREAM, FOR GARNISH

8 CHESTNUT PIECES, FOR GARNISH (OPTIONAL)

GLASSWARE

8 IRISH COFFEE MUGS (SEE PAGE 23)

Place the milk, sugar, cinnamon, and salt in a large saucepan over medium heat. Cook, stirring regularly, until the mixture is hot, about 5 minutes.

Add the chocolate and cook, stirring constantly, until the chocolate has melted completely.

Add the chestnut puree and cook, stirring constantly, until the puree is completely incorporated.

Stir in the liquors, if desired. Ladle into the mugs, top with whipped cream—and a chestnut piece, if desired—and serve.

HOT CHOCOLATE
CHOCOLATE

MAKES SIX 10-OUNCE SERVINGS

This favorite recipe is named chocolate twice because it uses both cocoa powder and whole chocolate. Don't think this recipe is for kids only; end a winter dinner party with mugs full of hot chocolate and a plate of biscotti. The molasses adds a slightly smoky, spicy richness, and Marshmallow Fluff makes a great and unexpectedly smooth topping.

48 OUNCES MILK

6 TABLESPOONS COCOA POWDER

3 TABLESPOONS CONFECTIONERS' SUGAR

1 TEASPOON VANILLA EXTRACT

1 TEASPOON MOLASSES

SCANT ⅛ TEASPOON SALT

9 OUNCES DARK OR MILK CHOCOLATE, CHOPPED INTO SMALL PIECES

6 SUPER-HEAPING TABLESPOONS WHIPPED CREAM OR MARSHMALLOW FLUFF

6 CINNAMON STICKS, FOR GARNISH

GLASSWARE

6 COFFEE CUPS
or
6 IRISH COFFEE MUGS
(SEE PAGE 23)

Place the milk, cocoa powder, confectioners' sugar, vanilla, molasses, and salt in a large saucepan over medium heat. Cook, whisking constantly, until the mixture is hot, about 5 minutes.

Add the chocolate and cook, stirring constantly, until the chocolate has melted completely, 5 to 10 minutes.

Remove from the heat and pour into coffee cups or mugs. Top with the whipped cream or Fluff, stir with a cinnamon stick, and serve.

CHRISTMAS EVE CHOCOLATE

MAKES FOURTEEN 2-OUNCE SERVINGS

When I was growing up, my friend Steve Santaniello's mother threw the best Christmas Eve parties in the neighborhood. This high-octane drink, a cross between hot chocolate and coffee, was always served around ten o'clock so we would be sure to be awake at midnight to ring in Christmas Day.

12 OUNCES STRONG BLACK COFFEE OR ESPRESSO

8 OUNCES DARK CHOCOLATE, CHOPPED INTO SMALL PIECES

¼ CUP SUGAR

3 OUNCES KAHLÚA

3 OUNCES DARK CRÈME DE CACAO

2 OUNCES GRAPPA OR BRANDY

WHIPPED CREAM, FOR GARNISH (OPTIONAL)

GLASSWARE

14 ESPRESSO CUPS OR SMALL COFFEE CUPS

In a medium saucepan over medium heat, combine the coffee, chocolate, and sugar. Cook, stirring constantly, until the chocolate has completely melted and the mixture is steaming hot.

Add the liquors and continue to heat, stirring well, for 1 minute.

Serve in espresso cups, topped, if desired, with a dollop of whipped cream.

CHAPTER
-**6**-

AFTER-
DINNER
DRINKS

RUSHING RIGHT INTO DESSERT after a large meal leaves many people uncomfortably full. I much prefer to clear everything away and tidy up the kitchen. Then I can relax with my guests over an after-dinner drink. In many cases the drink itself is dessert—or at least as much a part of dessert as the accompanying cookies, dried fruits, chocolates, or nuts.

CHOOSE THE AFTER-DINNER beverage based on what is served during the meal. If dinner is rich and heavy, serve a light after-dinner cocktail, such as the Grand Galliano (page 113). If the meal is lighter, serve a richer after-dinner beverage such as the Blackberry Caramel (page 116). This way you'll neither overstuff your guests nor leave them wanting more.

GRAND GALLIANO

This is a more adult version of a Creamsicle. It calls for Galliano, an Italian liqueur made from unaged grape brandy and many different herbs. If you have the stamina, shake it until you can't shake anymore. The result will be an ethereally light cocktail perfect for a slow-sipping nightcap. Served over crushed ice, it makes a wonderful frappé.

2 OUNCES GALLIANO

2 OUNCES GRAND MARNIER

2 OUNCES HEAVY CREAM

2 ORANGE TWISTS (SEE PAGE 66), FOR GARNISH

GLASSWARE

2 COCKTAIL GLASSES
(SEE PAGE 20)

Fill a cocktail shaker with ice and add the Galliano, Grand Marnier, and cream. Shake vigorously until the outside of the shaker is beaded with sweat and frosty.

Strain into the cocktail glasses, garnish each with an orange twist, and serve.

CHOCOLATE-COVERED CHERRY

MAKES TWO 3-OUNCE DRINKS

I first experienced this combination of flavors served as a shooter, which is a shot, or small drink, that you gulp down in one go. I quickly realized what a delight a slow-sipping version would be for lovers of chocolate-covered cherries.

3 OUNCES CHERRY HEERING
OR CHERRY BRANDY

3 OUNCES DARK CRÈME DE CACAO

2 MARASCHINO CHERRIES

GLASSWARE

2 COCKTAIL GLASSES
(SEE PAGE 20)

Fill a pitcher with ice and add the Cherry Heering and crème de cacao. Stir briskly until the outside of the pitcher is beaded with sweat and frosty.

Strain into the cocktail glasses, garnish each with a cherry, and serve.

BLACKBERRY CARAMEL

This is a great cocktail to serve alongside strong coffee. Frangelico is an Italian liqueur made from hazelnuts. It is light and delicate compared to other cordials and has a dry—as opposed to cloying—finish. It is wonderful to drink on its own and is fabulous as a mixer.

4 OUNCES ECHTE KROATZBEERE BLACKBERRY LIQUEUR

4 OUNCES FRANGELICO

2 OUNCES BRANDY

2 OUNCES CREAM

2 TEASPOONS BROWN SUGAR SYRUP (PAGE 71)

4 BLACKBERRIES, FOR GARNISH

GLASSWARE

4 COCKTAIL GLASSES (SEE PAGE 20)

Fill a pitcher with ice and add the blackberry liqueur, Frangelico, brandy, cream, and brown sugar syrup. Stir vigorously until the outside of the pitcher is beaded with sweat and frosty.

Strain into the cocktail glasses, garnish each drink with a blackberry, and serve.

MOCHA RUM TODDY

MAKES FOUR 6-OUNCE DRINKS

This flavorful toddy is based on a natural combination of rich coffee and creamy, molasses-based dark rum. For warm and spicy undertones, add a teaspoon of cocoa powder to the coffee grounds before brewing the coffee.

4 TEASPOONS SUGAR (OPTIONAL)

16 OUNCES FRESHLY BREWED COFFEE

4 OUNCES DARK CRÈME DE CACAO

4 OUNCES DARK RUM

1 CUP WHIPPED CREAM

1 TEASPOON COCOA POWDER, FOR GARNISH

GLASSWARE

4 IRISH COFFEE MUGS (SEE PAGE 23)

Add the sugar, if using, to the hot coffee and stir until dissolved. Stir in the crème de cacao and rum.

Pour the coffee into the mugs. Top each serving with ¼ cup whipped cream and ¼ teaspoon cocoa and serve.

CAFÉ FRAPPÉ

Coffee works particularly well as a frappé, where the bitterness inherent in coffee is made milder by crushed ice. In this version, well-sweetened coffee is spiked with brandy for a smooth drink with a bit of buzz.

4 TEASPOONS SUGAR

12 OUNCES FRESHLY BREWED FRENCH ROAST COFFEE

4 OUNCES BRANDY

CRUSHED ICE, FOR SERVING

GLASSWARE

4 ROCKS GLASSES
(SEE PAGE 19)

Add the sugar to the hot coffee. Stir well and let cool to room temperature, about 30 minutes, or refrigerate for 15 minutes.

Add the brandy to the cooled coffee.

Fill the rocks glasses with crushed ice, fill with the coffee mixture, and serve.

PLANNING AHEAD
Brew the coffee at least 30 minutes before serving and allow it to come to room temperature, or make it up to 8 hours ahead and store in the refrigerator.

CAFÉ BRÛLOT

MAKES SIX 7-OUNCE DRINKS

This New Orleans classic typically calls for igniting the liquor and allowing it to burn off. I don't recommend doing this unless you are well practiced in flambéing food.

8 OUNCES BRANDY

4 OUNCES GRAND MARNIER

¼ CUP SUGAR

4 CINNAMON STICKS, CRACKED INTO SEVERAL LARGE PIECES

TWISTS FROM 1 ORANGE (SEE PAGE 66)

32 OUNCES FRESHLY BREWED DARK ROAST COFFEE

GLASSWARE

6 COFFEE CUPS
or
6 IRISH COFFEE MUGS
(SEE PAGE 23)

Place the brandy, Grand Marnier, sugar, cinnamon sticks, and orange twists in a heavy-bottomed saucepan over medium-high heat. Warm the mixture until hot. Using a slotted spoon, remove the cinnamon sticks and orange twists.

Add the coffee and stir well.

Ladle into coffee cups or mugs and serve.

VARIATION

....

Spicy Café Brûlot: To make the coffee even richer and spicier, brew it with 2 ounces of chicory added to the coffee grounds. Also try replacing 1 cinnamon stick with 1 whole star anise for a slightly more exotic flavor.

RESOURCES

For bitters, syrups, and mixes:
Fee Brothers
800-961-FEES (800-961-3337)
feebrothers.com

For Peychaud's bitters
and rums:
The Sazerac Company
866-729-3722
sazerac.com

For cocktail mixes
and syrups:
Trader Vic's
925-675-6400
tradervics.com

For bar supplies,
top to bottom:
Cocktail Kingdom
212-647-9166
cocktailkingdom.com

For a diverse selection of bar
supplies—jiggers, stirrers,
mixing glasses, you name it:
Bar Supplies
barsupplies.com

For spices:
BulkFoods.com
419-537-1713
bulkfoods.com

For spices and dried herbs:
Penzeys Spices
800-741-7787
penzeys.com

For dried fruits, nuts,
and preserves:
American Spoon
888-735-6700
spoon.com

For a broad range of spices,
dried herbs, and flavorings,
including rose water and
orange flower water:
The Spice House
312-676-2414
thespicehouse.com

For all sorts of things, from
bar supplies to paper supplies
to juices:
Food Service Direct
757-245-7675
foodservicedirect.com

For lime juice and
other specialties:
Nellie and Joe's
800-LIME-PIE (800-546-3743)
keylimejuice.com

For lemon juice and
other specialties:
Melissa's
800-588-0151
melissas.com

For quality syrups
and mixers, coffees, and
specialty ingredients:
Aroma Ridge
800-JAVA-123 (800-528-2123)
aromaridge.com

For superior coffees with
high-quality organics:
Kobrick Coffee Co.
800-562-7491
kobricks.com

For cacao nibs, cocoa powder,
and other chocolate items:
Scharffen Berger Chocolate
Maker
855-972-0511
scharffenberger.com

For caper berries and
all sorts of specialty
ingredients:
Scandinavian Spice
877-783-7626
scandinavianspice.com

For sea salts from
all over the world:
SaltWorks
425-885-7258
seasalt.com

For glassware:
Ravenscroft Crystal
212-463-9834 (wholesale)
ravenscroftcrystal.com

INDEX

Note: Page numbers in *italics* refer to illustrations.

after-dinner drinks, 110–21
  Blackberry Caramel, 116
  Café Brûlot, 120, *121*
  Café Frappé, *118*, 119
  Chocolate-Covered Cherry, 114, *115*
  Grand Galliano, *112*, 113
  Mocha Rum Toddy, 117
  Spicy Café Brûlot, 120
Angostura bitters, 31
Apple Crush, 74–75
applejack:
  Apple Crush, 74–75
  Pumpkin Cider, 96, *97*
Apricot Mulled Wine, *102*, 103–4
Armagnac, 28
Autumn Punch, 36–37

balance, 12
Banana Butter, 93, 95
Banana Buttered Rum, 93–95, *94*
Banana Rum Punch, 41–42, *43*
Battista, Iris, 90
bitters, 31
Blackberry Caramel, 116
Blood Orange Sparkler, 52, *53*
Boston shaker, 13–14
bourbon, 26
  Dry Manhattan, 66
  General Washington's Grog, 92
  Grape and Grain, *78*, 79
  Holiday Eggnog, *84*, 85–86
  Manhattan, *64*, 65
  Mint Julep, 69, *70*
  Old-Fashioned, 68
  Perfect Manhattan, 67
  Thanksgiving Nog, 87–88, *89*
  Whiskey and Ginger Punch, 40
brandy, 27–28
  Blackberry Caramel, 116
  Brandywine Sour, *58*, 59
  Café Brûlot, 120, *121*
  Café Frappé, *118*, 119
  Chestnut Hot Chocolate, 105
  Christmas Eve Chocolate, *108*, 109

French 75, *50*, 51
  Holiday Eggnog, *84*, 85–86
  Old-Fashioned, 68
  Park Avenue, 55
  Thanksgiving Nog, 87–88, *89*
Brown Sugar Syrup, 71
bubblies, 44–61
  Blood Orange Sparkler, 52, *53*
  Brandywine Sour, *58*, 59
  Cherry Sugar Fizz, *46*, 47
  French 75, *50*, 51
  Kir Royale, 54
  Magnificent Mimosa, 48, *49*
  Park Avenue, 55
  Pear, Poire, 61
  Thanksgiving Sparkler, 56–57
Buttered Rum, 95

Café Brûlot, 120, *121*
Café Frappé, *118*, 119
Calvados, 29
  Apple Crush, 74–75
  Pumpkin Cider, 96, *97*
Candied Grapefruit Peel, 36–37
Champagne, 45
  see also wine, sparkling
channel knives, 15
cherries:
  Chocolate-Covered Cherry, 114, *115*
  Maraschino Muddle, 80, *81*
Cherry Sugar Fizz, *46*, 47
Chestnut Hot Chocolate, 105
chocolate:
  Chestnut Hot Chocolate, 105
  Chocolate-Covered Cherry, 114, *115*
  Christmas Eve Chocolate, *108*, 109
  Hot Chocolate Chocolate, 106, *107*
  Mocha Rum Toddy, 117
Christmas Eve Chocolate, *108*, 109
cider:
  Hot Spiked Cider, *98*, 99
  Pumpkin Cider, 96, *97*
citrus bitters, 31
classic cocktails, 62–81
  Apple Crush, 74–75
  Dry Manhattan, 66
  Grape and Grain, *78*, 79

Manhattan, *64*, 65
Maraschino Muddle, 80, *81*
Mint Julep, 69, *70*
Old-Fashioned, 68
Pear Cobbler, 72, 73
Perfect Manhattan, 67
Rosmarino, 76–77, *77*
cobbler shaker, 13
cocktail spoons, 14
coffee:
    Café Brûlot, 120, *121*
    Café Frappé, *118*, 119
    Christmas Eve Chocolate, *108*, 109
    Iris's Coffee Nog, 90–91
    Mocha Rum Toddy, 117
    Spicy Café Brûlot, 120
Cognac, 28
Crème Anglaise, 85–86, 90–91
Crème de Cacao:
    Chocolate-Covered Cherry, 114, *115*
    Christmas Eve Chocolate, *108*, 109
    Mocha Rum Toddy, 117
Curaçao, 30

Drunken Fruit, 99
Dry Manhattan, 66

Eggnog, Holiday, *84*, 85–86

Fig Mulled Wine, 100–101
floating, 18
Frangelico:
    Blackberry Caramel, 116
Chestnut Hot Chocolate, 105
French 75, *50*, 51

Galliano: Grand Galliano, *112*, 113
General Washington's Grog, 92
gin, 25
    French 75, *50*, 51
ginger: Whiskey and Ginger Punch, 40
glassware, 19–23
Grand Galliano, *112*, 113
Grand Marnier:
    Café Brûlot, 120, *121*
    Grand Galliano, *112*, 113
Grape and Grain, *78*, 79
Grapefruit Peel, Candied, 36–37
grappa: Christmas Eve Chocolate, *108*, 109

Holiday Eggnog, *84*, 85–86

home bar basics:
    balance, 12
    bitters, 31
    booze, 24–30
    glassware, 19–23
    measurements, 32–33
    techniques, 17–18
    tools, 13–16

Irish whiskey, 25
Iris's Coffee Nog, 90–91

jiggers, 14
juicers, 16

Kahlúa:
    Christmas Eve Chocolate, *108*, 109
    Iris's Coffee Nog, 90–91
Kir Royale, 54
knives, 15

Lemon Sour Mix, 60
Lemon Swirls, 54
Lime Sour Mix, 60

Madeira: General Washington's Grog, 92
Manhattan, *64*, 65
    Dry Manhattan, 66
    Perfect Manhattan, 67
Maraschino Muddle, 80, *81*
measurements, 32–33
Mimosa, Magnificent, 48, *49*
Mint Julep, 69, *70*
Mocha Rum Toddy, 117
muddlers, 15
muddling, 18

nogs, grogs & warmers, 82–109
    Apricot Mulled Wine, *102*, 103–4
    Banana Buttered Rum, 93–95, *94*
    Chestnut Hot Chocolate, 105
    Christmas Eve Chocolate, *108*, 109
    Fig Mulled Wine, 100–101
    General Washington's Grog, 92
    Holiday Eggnog, *84*, 85–86
    Hot Chocolate Chocolate, 106, *107*
    Hot Spiked Cider, *98*, 99
    Iris's Coffee Nog, 90–91
    Pumpkin Cider, 96, *97*
    Thanksgiving Nog, 87–88, *89*
nutmeg grater, 15

Old-Fashioned, 68
orange juice: Magnificent Mimosa, 48, *49*

Park Avenue, 55
Pear, Poire, 61
Pear Cobbler, 72, *73*
Perfect Manhattan, 67
Pernod: Rosmarino, 76–77, *77*
Peychaud's bitters, 31
pitchers, 16
Pomegranate Punch, *38*, 39
pumpkin:
    Pumpkin Cider, 96, *97*
    Thanksgiving Nog, 87–88, *89*
punches, 34–43
    Autumn Punch, 36–37
    Banana Rum Punch, 41–42, *43*
    Pomegranate Punch, *38*, 39
    Whiskey and Ginger Punch, 40

reamers, 16
Red Wine Syrup, 71
rimming, 18
Rosmarino, 76–77, *77*
rum, 26–27
    Banana Buttered Rum, 93–95, *94*
    Banana Rum Punch, 41–42, *43*
    Buttered Rum, 95
    General Washington's Grog, 92
    Holiday Eggnog, *84*, 85–86
    Hot Spiked Cider, *98*, 99
    Iris's Coffee Nog, 90–91
    Mocha Rum Toddy, 117
    Thanksgiving Nog, 87–88, *89*
rye whiskey, 26
    Dry Manhattan, 66
    Manhattan, *64*, 65
    Old-Fashioned, 68
    Perfect Manhattan, 67

Santaniello, Steve, 109
Scotch, 26
    Old-Fashioned, 68
shakers, 13–14
shaking, 17
sherry: Autumn Punch, 36–37
Simple Syrup, 71
    Brown Sugar Syrup, 71
    Red Wine Syrup, 71

Sour Mix, 60
Spanish brandy, 29
Spicy Café Brûlot, 120
stirring, 17
strainers, 14

techniques, 17–18
    floating, 18
    muddling, 18
    rimming, 18
    shaking and stirring, 17
tequila, 27
Thanksgiving Nog, 87–88, *89*
Thanksgiving Sparkler, 56–57
topping: Fig Wine Topping, 101
Triple Sec: Pear Cobbler, 72, *73*

vermouth, 29
vermouth, dry:
    Dry Manhattan, 66
    Rosmarino, 76–77, *77*
vermouth, sweet:
    Blood Orange Sparkler, 52, *53*
    Manhattan, *64*, 65
    Perfect Manhattan, 67
vodka, 24
    Apple Crush, 74–75
    Pomegranate Punch, *38*, 39
    Rosemary-Infused Vodka, 76
    Rosmarino, 76–77, *77*

whiskey, 25–26
Whiskey and Ginger Punch, 40
wine:
    Apricot Mulled Wine, *102*, 103–4
    Brandywine Sour, *58*, 59
    Fig Mulled Wine, 100–101
    Red Wine Syrup, 71
wine, sparkling:
    Blood Orange Sparkler, 52, *53*
    Cherry Sugar Fizz, *46*, 47
    French 75, *50*, 51
    Kir Royale, 54
    Magnificent Mimosa, 48, *49*
    Park Avenue, 55
    Pear, Poire, 61
    Thanksgiving Sparkler, 56–57

zesters, 15

CONVERSION CHARTS

Here are rounded-off equivalents between the metric system and the traditional systems that are used in the United States to measure weight and volume.

FRACTIONS	DECIMALS
1/8	.125
1/4	.25
1/3	.33
3/8	.375
1/2	.5
5/8	.625
2/3	.67
3/4	.75
7/8	.875

WEIGHTS

US/UK	METRIC
1/4 oz	7 g
1/2 oz	15 g
1 oz	30 g
2 oz	55 g
3 oz	85 g
4 oz	110 g
5 oz	140 g
6 oz	170 g
7 oz	200 g
8 oz (1/2 lb)	225 g
9 oz	250 g
10 oz	280 g
11 oz	310 g
12 oz	340 g
13 oz	370 g
14 oz	400 g
15 oz	425 g
16 oz (1 lb)	455 g

VOLUME

AMERICAN	IMPERIAL	METRIC
1/4 tsp		1.25 ml
1/2 tsp		2.5 ml
1 tsp		5 ml
1/2 Tbsp (1 1/2 tsp)		7.5 ml
1 Tbsp (3 tsp)		15 ml
1/4 cup (4 Tbsp)	2 fl oz	60 ml
1/3 cup (5 Tbsp)	2 1/2 fl oz	75 ml
1/2 cup (8 Tbsp)	4 fl oz	125 ml
2/3 cup (10 Tbsp)	5 fl oz	150 ml
3/4 cup (12 Tbsp)	6 fl oz	175 ml
1 cup (16 Tbsp)	8 fl oz	250 ml
1 1/4 cups	10 fl oz	300 ml
1 1/2 cups	12 fl oz	350 ml
2 cups (1 pint)	16 fl oz	500 ml
2 1/2 cups	20 fl oz (1 pint)	625 ml
5 cups	40 fl oz (1 qt)	1.25 l

OVEN TEMPERATURES

	°F	°C	GAS MARK
very cool	250–275	130–140	1/2–1
cool	300	148	2
warm	325	163	3
moderate	350	177	4
moderately hot	375–400	190–204	5–6
hot	425	218	7
very hot	450–475	232–245	8–9

°C/F TO °F/C CONVERSION CHART

°C/F	°C	°F	°C/F	°C	°F	°C/F	°C	°F	°C/F	°C	°F
90	32	194	220	104	428	350	177	662	480	249	896
100	38	212	230	110	446	360	182	680	490	254	914
110	43	230	240	116	464	370	188	698	500	260	932
120	49	248	250	121	482	380	193	716	510	266	950
130	54	266	260	127	500	390	199	734	520	271	968
140	60	284	270	132	518	400	204	752	530	277	986
150	66	302	280	138	536	410	210	770	540	282	1,004
160	71	320	290	143	554	420	216	788	550	288	1,022
170	77	338	300	149	572	430	221	806			
180	82	356	310	154	590	440	227	824			
190	88	374	320	160	608	450	232	842			
200	93	392	330	166	626	460	238	860			
210	99	410	340	171	644	470	243	878			

Example: If your temperature is 90°F, your conversion is 32°C; if your temperature is 90°C, your conversion is 194°F.

Library of Congress Cataloging-in-Publication Data

Names: Mautone, Nick, author.
Title: The artisanal kitchen. Holiday cocktails / Nick Mautone.
Other titles: Holiday cocktails
Description: New York, NY : Artisan, a division of Workman Publishing Co., Inc. [2017] |
    Includes bibliographical references and index.
Identifiers: LCCN 2017005099 | ISBN 9781579658038 (paper-over-board)
Subjects: LCSH: Cocktails. | LEGF: Cookbooks.
Classification: LCC TX951 .M3185 2017 | DDC 641.87/4—dc23
LC record available at https://lccn.loc.gov/2017005099

Cover design by Erica Heitman-Ford
Cover photographs by Lauren Volo
Design by Erica Heitman-Ford

Artisan books are available at special discounts when purchased in bulk for premiums and sales promotions as well as for fund-raising or educational use. Special editions or book excerpts also can be created to specification. For details, contact the Special Sales Director at the address below, or send an e-mail to specialmarkets@workman.com.

Published by Artisan
A division of Workman Publishing Co., Inc.
225 Varick Street
New York, NY 10014-4381
artisanbooks.com

Artisan is a registered trademark of Workman Publishing Co., Inc.

This book has been adapted from *Raising the Bar* (Artisan, 2004).

Published simultaneously in Canada by Thomas Allen & Son, Limited

Printed in China

First printing, September 2017

10 9 8 7 6 5 4 3 2 1